Deep Learning in
Practice

Deep Learning in Practice

Mehdi Ghayoumi

Cornell University

CRC Press is an imprint of the
Taylor & Francis Group, an **informa** business

First edition published 2022
by CRC Press
6000 Broken Sound Parkway NW, Suite 300, Boca Raton, FL 33487-2742

and by CRC Press
2 Park Square, Milton Park, Abingdon, Oxon, OX14 4RN

CRC Press is an imprint of Taylor & Francis Group, LLC

© 2022 Mehdi Ghayoumi

Library of Congress Cataloging-in-Publication Data
Names: Ghayoumi, Mehdi, author.
Title: Deep learning in practice / Mehdi Ghayoumi.
Description: First edition. | Boca Raton : CRC Press, 2022. | Includes
  bibliographical references and index.
Identifiers: LCCN 2021030250 | ISBN 9780367458621 (hardback) | ISBN
  9780367456580 (paperback) | ISBN 9781003025818 (ebook)
Subjects: LCSH: Deep learning (Machine learning)
Classification: LCC Q325.73 .G43 2022 | DDC 006.3/1--dc23
LC record available at https://lccn.loc.gov/2021030250

ISBN: 978-0-367-45862-1 (hbk)
ISBN: 978-0-367-45658-0 (pbk)
ISBN: 978-1-003-02581-8 (ebk)

DOI: 10.1201/9781003025818

Typeset in Minion
by SPi Technologies India Pvt Ltd (Straive)

Front cover image: One of the applications of Deep Learning is to create new things (objects, faces, image, dreams, etc.) that do not exist. The cover image has been designed in that spirit.

Contents

Preface

DEEP LEARNING IS ONE OF THE MOST RECENT and advanced topics in machine learning, with several applications in many fields. It shows promising results in many areas, from computer vision to drug discovery and stock market prediction. There are many books and articles in deep learning that discuss its algorithms, theories, and applications. Also, because of its capabilities and potentials in solving different problems by deploying different data types, many researchers and people who are not in computer science or related fields are interested in learning and using deep learning architectures in their projects.

This book – **Deep Learning in Practice** – reviews the fundamentals and concepts that a person (who is new in machine learning and deep learning) needs to learn to start and implement a new project in deep learning. It is a practical book with many programming code examples and figures to help you understand the concepts better. The book presents some reviews on the most required topics in python, NumPy, TensorFlow, and Keras to implement a deep learning project. Next, the book reviews the fundamentals of artificial neural networks and some most popular and exciting deep learning algorithms. Chapter 7 presents a project that deploys some methods and algorithms presented in the book to implement a virtual assistant robot. The final chapter gives you a guideline to explore the most optimized model for your project.

I would expect this book's contents to be welcomed worldwide by undergraduate and graduate students and researchers in deep learning, including practitioners in academia and industry. Furthermore, I hope that readers would find the presented chapters in this book interesting and inspiring to learn more advanced concepts (theoretical and practical viewpoints) and discovering more secrets of deep learning.

Mehdi Ghayoumi
Los Angeles, CA, USA
August, 2021

Acknowledgments

I WANT TO THANK MY FAMILY MOST OF ALL. Some days I felt as though I would not finish this book without their supports and encouragement.

Thank you to all the friends and colleagues who shared their feedbacks and gave their supports and inspiration throughout this book's writing.

Most importantly, this book would not be possible without the wishes, love, and supports of my mother, Khadijeh Ghayoumi.

This book is dedicated to the soul of my kind-hearted father, Aliasghar Ghayoumi, and my loving mother, Khadijeh Ghayoumi.

Author

Dr. Mehdi Ghayoumi is a course facilitator at Cornell University and adjunct faculty of Computer Science at the University of San Diego. Prior to this, he was a research assistant professor at SUNY at Binghamton, where he was the Media Core Lab's dynamic leader. He was also a lecturer at Kent State University, where he received the Teaching Award for two consecutive years in 2016 and 2017. In addition, he has been teaching machine learning, data science, robotic and programming courses for several years.

Dr. Ghayoumi research interests are in Machine Learning, Machine Vision, Robotics, and Human-Robot Interaction (HRI). His research focuses are on building real systems for realistic environment settings, and his current projects have applications in Human-Robot Interaction, manufacturing, biometric, and healthcare.

He is a technical program committee member of several conferences, workshops, and editorial board member of several journals in machine learning, mathematics, and robotics, like ICML, ICPR, HRI, FG, WACV, IROS, CIBCB, and JAI. In addition, his research papers have been published at conferences and journals in the fields, including **Human-Computer Interaction (HRI)**, **R**obotics **S**cience and **S**ystems **(RSS)**, International Conference on Machine Learning and Applications **(ICMLA)**, and others.

## CHAPTER 1

Introduction

1.1 WHAT IS LEARNING?

There are several definitions for learning, and maybe we can say, "Learning is the achievement of knowledge or skills through study or getting experience." Humans need to promote their social and personal situations and conditions to make their life better. For this purpose, in every moment, people face a decision-making situation. For everyone, getting new knowledge and learning new skills help make better decisions and help people be more successful in their personal and professional life. There are several research and studies to know about the humans learning process. One of the most important parts of these research and studies is discovering how learning can be simulated in machines and how it can be more accurate and effective.

1.2 WHAT IS MACHINE LEARNING?

Nowadays and through the last decades, machines help a lot to make human life more comfortable. One challenge that humans always like to solve is making machines smarter to assist humans better, and researchers are working on this goal and trying to find methods to make machines smarter than before. These methods and research are included in machine learning, as one of the areas in computer science that recently got the most interest from people who are working in the academy and industry. Many algorithms and methods have discovered and developed in this field: some traditional ones like **Support Vector Machine (SVM)** or **Decision Tree (DT)**, and some new one like **Deep Learning (DL)**.

DOI: 10.1201/9781003025818-1

1.3 WHAT IS DEEP LEARNING?

One of the research methods in artificial intelligence is to imitate human behavior, like human learning to build systems that can learn. Therefore, the researchers in this field try to find methods and design algorithms that imitate human learning. For this purpose, researchers and engineers started to research to understand how machines can learn to make their functionalities smarter. **Artificial Neural Networks (ANNs)** are the most famous examples of these attempts. For instance, the perceptron (one of the first ANNs methods) imitates the human's neural network formation and processes. It is used as the base of some advanced ANNs methods like deep learning (DL).

DL is one of the recent and advanced machine learning algorithms. Its methods showed fascinating results in many areas, especially in the applications where their data are image and audio. It simulates the learning style in the human brain. Its name is deep because of using several layers and deploying more details of the data features for learning. Its structure in total has three parts: input, output, and hidden layers. The outputs depend on several parameters in architecture like: the neurons' combination in each layer, weights, bias, and activation function. All the learning process steps occur in two main stages: finding a model by transforming data to a linear or nonlinear model and then improving the model.

1.4 ABOUT THIS BOOK!

This book reviews the fundamentals of DL algorithms and presents the main DL methods with some examples. It has been designed to give you some information about the DL methods and algorithms and, in the end, presents several projects to help you learn and know how to implement your project. We have less focus on the math and the theory parts of DL in this book and show you how to use the DL algorithm in real-world projects. The book is suitable for people who would like to start using DL in their projects. The book has eight chapters to cover these goals as follows:

1.4.1 Introduction

This chapter (current chapter) reviews the book chapters and gives brief descriptions of each chapter's contents.

1.4.2 Python/NumPy

Python is one of the most interesting programming languages with several libraries for many applications, and it is easy to learn. Also, NumPy has some features (especially for arrays and matrices) that make the computation faster and easier. This book has a quick review of these tools to help reader to understand the projects better.

1.4.3 TensorFlow and Keras Fundamentals

TensorFlow is one of the most famous platforms for DL presented by Google. This book has a quick review on this platform with some examples to learn how to define the tensors and ease implementations. We also have a quick review of Keras with examples.

1.4.4 Artificial Neural Networks (ANNs) Fundamentals and Architectures

For learning DL better, you should know the fundamentals of artificial neural networks. We review some basics of ANNs architectures and present the famous ANNs with examples using TensorFlow and Keras.

1.4.5 Deep Neural Networks (DNNs) Fundamentals and Architectures

This chapter provides the fundamentals of DL and gives some examples of the most famous and popular DL architectures and their applications. It gives you the essential tips that you need to know when you plan to start using DL in your projects.

1.4.6 Deep Neural Networks for Images and Audio Data Analysis

Image and audio data analysis is one of the most common applications of DL. DL showed very promising results in the projects in which their data are image or audio. This chapter provides examples to teach you how to use CNN (as one of the DL methods we discuss later) for visual and audio data.

1.4.7 Deep Neural Networks for Virtual Assistant Robots

This chapter provides the details to implement a virtual assistant robot as a project that deploys several DL architectures in different project modules, like face recognition, speech recognition, and sentiment analysis. Some example codes for each of these modules help you to learn better.

In addition, it helps you to know how to implement a real-world project using different DL algorithms.

1.4.8 Finding the Best Model?

This chapter shows the steps to learn how to find the best model from the first trained model. Finding the best model is one of the challenging problems in machine learning, and here we have a quick review to know how we can optimize the model and evaluate it.

## CHAPTER 2

Python/NumPy Fundamentals

2.1 PYTHON

2.1.1 Variables

A place of the memory to store data. It has a name to access it or change it. The syntax is:

```
variable = expression
```

There are four main types of variables.

TABLE 2.1   Data Types in Python

Type	Example 1	Example 2	Example 3
Integers	30	0	−10
Real number	3.14	0.0	−3.14
Strings	"Hello"	""	"77"
Boolean	True	False	

Python can recognize the type of data when you assign it to the variable. There are some conversion functions like int, float, str, and bool to change the type of data. For example, a conversion command converts the integer to the new data type when the type is an integer. For example, str (30) ➜ 30, at first, the type of the 30 is an integer, and after conversion, the type of 30 is a string. Naming variables is based on these rules:

1. It can contain only numbers, letters, and underscores.

2. It cannot start with a number.

DOI: 10.1201/9781003025818-2

3. It is cAsE-sEnSiTiVe.

4. It uses camelCase.

5. It never contains spaces.

6. It often uses underscore in names with multiple words.

If you don't follow these rules, you will get some errors. In your module and projects, the variable name should have some meaning related to its values (it is better to choose descriptive names).

2.1.2 Keywords

You cannot use keywords for naming variables. However, you can remember these words, or have their list when the interpreter gives you an error and then check the list.

TABLE 2.2   Keywords in Python

Reserved Keywords in Python					
and	as	assert	break	class	continue
def	del	elif	else	except	exec
finally	for	from	global	if	import
in	is	lambda	nonlocal	not	or
pass	raise	return	try	while	with
yield	True	False	None		

2.1.3 Operators and Operand

The special symbols we use for computation are operators, and the values that they work on are operand. There are several types of operation for data types as follows:

TABLE 2.3   Operators and their Operations

Operator	Description	Example	Evaluates to
+	addition	7 + 3	10
−	subtraction	7–3	4
*	multiplication	7 * 3	21
/	division (True)	7 / 3	2.333333
//	division (Integer)	7 // 3	2
%	modulus	7 % 3	1
**	exponent	7 ** 3	343

Also, there is a precedence order for operators as follows:

TABLE 2.4   Precedence Orders

Category	Example
Parentheses (grouping)	()
Exponent	a**b
Positive, negative	+a, −a
Multiplication, division, modulus	a * b, a / b, a // b, a % b
Addition, subtraction	a + b, a − b

There are also comparison operators that their outputs are Boolean values. Here are the comparison operators:

TABLE 2.5   Comparison Operators

Operator	Meaning	Sample Condition	Evaluates to
==	Equal to	5 == 5	True
!=	Not equal to	8!= 5	True
>	Greater than	3 > 10	False
<	Less than	5 < 8	True
>=	Greater than or equal to	5 >= 10	False
<=	Less than or equal to	5 <= 5	True

2.1.4 Statements and Expressions

An instruction that executes by the python interpreter is a statement. Some examples are as follows:

1. import statements,

2. assignment statement,

3. if statements,

4. for and while statements.

A combination of variables, operators, and values (also function) needs to be evaluated as an expression (interpreter print the results). Here the assignment is a statement, and there are two evaluations for **x** and **y**. With an assignment statement, like **x** = **7**, there is no evaluation (these are statements and just execute). Furthermore, its results create a reference from a variable. For example, **x** to **7**, and when we use a print function for **y** (everything in python is a function), we can see its value.

There are some methods like **input** function (it allows providing a prompt string) to get user data for making the program more interactive.

Example:

```
m = input ("Please enter your favorite number")
```

Here, after this line, the interpreter waits for the input value and puts the value in **m**.

The input returns string (even if the user puts the number). The solution is to convert the string to integer or float using **int** or **float** casting.

Example:

```
n=int (m)
print (n)
```

The type of **m** is string (even if the user enters the number), and the type of **n** is an integer. You cannot cast character to int or float. It is valid to assign variables several times (the current value is the last assigned value). The different variables can refer to the same place of the memory.

2.1.5 Sequence

A sequence is an "ordered set of things," Or "a group of items stored together in a collection."

Examples:

- a "range" of numbers,
- string variables,
- lists,
- tuples.

And the structures can be sequence or non-sequence.

- sequences (iterable types):
  - strings,
  - lists, dictionaries,

- non-sequences (non-iterable types):

  - boolean,

  - int, float.

2.1.6 For Loop

This technique allows us to repeat a block (set) of the codes for a specific time. It is a determined loop in which the programmer defines the loop iteration at the beginning of the code. Its syntax is as follows:

```
for a variable in sequence:
      # lines codes execute in every loop
            ...
 # lines code after the loop
    ...
```

In total, there are two types of **for**:

  a. for each (goes through every item in the sequence("iterable"))

  b. range-based for loop (goes through every item in a range)

for range (), these are the parameters:

```
range () generates a sequence of numbers based on some
parameters.
                    range (int start, int stop, int step)
start: begins at,
step: change each time,
stop: up to but not including.
```

There are three types for **range ()**:

- single parameter   range→ ending value,

- two parameters   range → starting value, ending value,

- three parameters   range→ starting value, ending value, and increment.

And there are two types of changes:

- positive increment moves forward,

- negative increment moves backward.

2.1.7 While Loop

It is an undetermined loop that its iteration checks in the block of the loop. This is the syntax:

(The block of the loop will continue until the conditions are true)

```
while condition:
            statements
        ...
```

2.1.8 String

The string is one of the data types that consist of some pieces, which are characters. It is a sequence of characters (there is an empty string if its length is zero). Mathematical operations do not work on strings even if their forms are like numbers (Except for + and *, which concatenates two strings and repetition). The characters can be accessed by their index. From left to right, it starts at **0**, and for accessing from right to left, it starts with **–1**. The string is an object in python that, same as other objects, has some methods. For example, upper and lower are the methods that convert a string to the uppercase and lowercase characters. Here are some string methods that are used more.

TABLE 2.6   Most Popular Methods for Strings

Method	Parameters	Description
upper	none	returns a string in all uppercase
lower	none	returns a string in all lowercase
capitalize	none	the first character is capitalized
strip	none	leading and trailing whitespace is removed
lstrip	none	leading whitespace is removed
rstrip	none	whitespace is removed
count	item	number of occurrences of an item
replace	old, new	replaces all occurrences of a substring
center	width	in a field of width return, a string centered
ljust	width	in a field of width, spaces return a string left-justified
rjust	width	in a field of width, spaces return a string right-justified
find	item	returns the leftmost index where substring item is found, or –1 if the item is not
index	item	if an item is not found, it is Like find except causes a runtime error

We use a comparison operator to compare strings. The outputs are true or false. Strings are immutable, and you cannot assign the values to the current space. However, you can play with the strings, for example, by using the + operator and a slice of string. You can traverse string by using loops and the items. Words **in** and **not in** are used to check if a string is a substring (even a single character is a substring) of another one.

2.1.9 List

It is a collection of the data (elements) that are indexed. It is like a string, but here the elements can be any type of data in python. For creating a list, you can use a square bracket []. You can access the list elements by using the index that it starts with **0**. You can also access using negative indexing like the string. You can use **in** and **not in** to check an element that exists or not in a list. + makes concatenation of two lists and * makes repetition of lists. There are the same concepts as the string for slicing. By using the **del**, you can remove elements from a list. You can use comparison operators either **is** or **is not** for making comparisons. You can use + and * on the list name as references to the list. There are some methods for lists that process the lists easier. Table 2.7 shows the methods that you can use when you are working with lists.

2.1.10 Dictionary

It is an unordered, changeable, and indexed collection. You can demonstrate it with curly brackets, and the key and values can represent its elements.

TABLE 2.7 Most Popular Methods for List

Method	Parameters	Result
append	Item	adding an item to the end
insert	position, item	inserts a new item at the position
pop	none	removes and then returns the last item of the list
pop	position	removes and then returns the item
sort	none	modifies to a sorted list
reverse	none	modifies in reverse order a list
index	item	returns the position of the first occurrence of an
count	item	returns the number of occurrences of an item
remove	item	removes the first occurrence of an item

Example:

```
mydict = {
    "python": "best",
    "Programming": "1",
    "language": 1999
}
print(mydict)
```

Output:

```
{'language': 1999, 'Programming': '1', 'python': 'best'}
```

You can access the dictionary values by putting the value of key or **get** ().

Example:

```
print(mydict["python"])
```

Output:

```
best
```

By using the key name, you can assign a new value to the key:

Example:

```
mydict["python"] =1999
print (mydict["python"])
```

Output:

```
1999
```

You can use the for loop to access the keys and values of a dictionary.

Example:

```
for x in mydict:
    print(x)
```

Output:

```
Programming
python
language
```

2.1.11 Tuple

A **tuple** is a python collection with these features: ordered, unchangeable, and you can demonstrate it with round brackets ().

Example:

```
mytuple = ("test", 7, "tuple")
print(mytuple)
```

Output:

```
('test', 7, 'tuple')
```

The instruction for indexing is the same as the list.

Example:

```
mytuple = ("test", 7, "tuple")
print(mytuple[-1])
```

Output:

```
tuple
```

The indexing range can be positive or negative. It has **start** (included) and **end** (is not included).

Example:

```
mytuple = ("test", 7, "tuple")
print(mytuple[1:3])
```

Output:

```
(7, 'tuple')
```

There is a trick to change the values of a tuple.

Example:

```
mytuple = ("test", 7, "tuple")
new_mytuple = list(mytuple)
new_mytuple[0] = "change"
mytuple = tuple(new_mytuple)
print(mytuple)
```

Output:

```
('change', 7, 'tuple')
```

You can access the tuple element using a loop.

Example:

```
mytuple = ("test", 7, "tuple")
for x in mytuple:
  print(x)
```

Output:

```
test
7
tuple
```

You cannot remove an item of a tuple, but you can delete it completely.

Example:

```
mytuple = ("test", 7, "tuple")
del mytuple
print(mytuple)
```

Output:

```
Traceback (most recent call last): File "./program.py",
line 3, in NameError: name 'mytuple' is not defined
```

You can add tuples to each other using + operator.

Example:

```
tuple1 = ("test")
tuple2 = ("7")
tuple3= ("tuple")
tuple4= tuple1 + tuple2+tuple3
print(tuple4)
```

Output:

```
test7tuple
```

You can use **if** and **in** to check an item exist in a tuple or not.

Example:

```
mytuple = ("test", 7, "tuple")
if "test" in mytuple:
  print ("Yes, the item is in the tuple")
```

Output:

```
Yes, the item is in the tuple
```

2.1.12 Sets

Set is a collection of data that has these features: unordered, unindexed, and written with curly brackets {}.

Example:

```
myset = {"test", 7, "set"}
print(myset)
```

Output:

```
{'test', 'set', 7}
```

You cannot access the elements of a set using an index because it is unordered and unindexed. However, you can use **for** loop for accessing set values.

Example:

```
myset = {"test", 7, "set"}
for x in myset:
  print(x)
```

Output:

```
set
test
7
```

For adding one item, you can use **add** ().

Example:

```
myset = {"test", 7, "set"}
myset.add("learning")
print(myset)
```

Output:

```
{'learning', 'test', 'set', 7}
```

For adding more than one item, you can use **update()**. We remove an item of a set by using **remove()** or **discard()**. The **remove()** raises an error if the item does not exist, but the **discard()** does not.

Example:

```
myset = {"test", 7, "set"}
myset.remove("test")
print(myset)
```

Output:

```
{'set', 7}'t', 7}
{'set', 7}'t', 7}
```

POP() removes the last item; however, because the set is unordered when you use **pop()**, you don't know which item exactly will be removed!

Example:

```
myset = {"test", 7, "set"}
myset.pop()
print(myset)
```

Output:

```
{'test', 7}
```

Clear() empties the set.

Example:

```
myset = {"test", 7, "set"}
myset.clear()
```

Output:

```
Set()
```

2.1.13 Function

A function is a block of the codes that do specific tasks. They are used to decrease computation costs. You can create it one time and use it anytime you need it by calling the function. Its syntax is as follows:

```
def name (parameters):

    statements
```

These are some functions that are built-in in python, and you can use them. You already used some of them (like print!). There are some libraries in python which, after importing them, we can use the library's methods and modules. Some functions return value. A function also can call other functions. You can call and execute all functions in the main function. It does not need any parameters. Python interpreter defines special variables (for example, __name__ that is automatically set to the string value "__main__") before executing the program.

2.1.14 File

It is a way to store the data. There are two tasks here, reading and writing, and there are two types of files, text, and binary. In python, we should open and close the file before and after we use it.

```
open(myfilename,'r')
```

Open a file called myfilename and use it for reading.

```
open(myfilename,'w')
```

Open a file called myfilename and use it for writing.

```
filevariable.close()
```

Assume there is a text file(test.txt). For reading the file at first, you should open the file and then read it. You can iterate file data using loop commands.

The syntax is as follows:

```
for line in myFile:
    statements
    ...
```

We can write to the file by opening a file, writing, and then closing it.

2.1.15 Object (class)

Python supports **Object-Oriented Programming (OOP)**. For each object, there are two main parts: states and methods. For creating an object, use the **class** keyword. Use the class name that you already created and then assign value to their parameters. For real-world application classes, every class has one __init__ function to initiate the class parameters. Methods are the functions that belong to the class. **Self** is an instance of the current object, and by using **self**, you can access the variables which belong to the class. You can use any name for **self** (here myobject). In addition, you can modify the properties of the object.

2.2 NUMPY

It is a python library that makes working with the array easier. Most of the data computations in deep learning algorithms are with an array, and NumPy can help us make them faster (however, the python list does the array computation, the NumPy module is up to 50 times faster). It uses the ndarray object and its modules for array processing.

After installing NumPy, it can be imported by:

```
import numpy as np
```

2.2.1 Create Array

For using an array by numpy, you should create it.

```
import numpy as np
a= np.array([1, 2, 3, 4])
```

2.2.2 ndarray

For creating a ndarray, we can pass datatypes like tuple or array into an array (), and then it will be converted to a ndarray. One of the key points here is the dimension value.

Look at these examples:

Example:

```
import numpy as np
# 0 Dimension
 arr0 = np.array(7)
# 1 Dimension
arr1 = np.array([5, 6, 7])
```

```
# 2 Dimension
arr2 = np.array([[1, 2, 3, 4], [5, 6, 7]])
# 3 Dimension
arr3 = np.array([[[10, 20, 30], [4, 5, 6, 7]], [[1, 2, 3],
[4, 5, 6, 7]]])
```

ndim gives us the dimension of the array.

Example:

```
print(arr1.ndim)
```

Output:

```
>>>1
```

2.2.3 Access Elements

You can access the array elements using an index. The first index is 0, and the second one is 1, etc. For accessing the array elements in 2D or ND array, you can separate the index by a comma for each dimension.

Example:

```
import numpy as np
arr1 = np.array([[[10, 20, 30, 40], [5, 6, 7, 8]],
[9, 10, 11, 12], [2, 3, 4, 5]])
print(myarr[0, 0, 2])
```

Output:

```
>>>30
```

Example:

The first index represents the first element in arr1:

```
arr2=[[1, 2, 3, 4], [5, 6, 7, 8]]
```

Example:

The second index represents the first element in arr2:

```
arr3=[1, 2, 3, 4]
```

Example:

The last index represents the third element in arr3:

3

2.2.4 Array Slicing

Here is the general syntax for slicing:

[start: end: step]

There are some default values:

start: zero, **end:** length of the array, **step:** 1

(This syntax is for a 1D array).
For more than 1D Array, before determining the start, end, and step, the array element that we plan to do slicing should be defined.

Example:

```
import numpy as np
myarr = np.array([10, 20, 30, 40, 50, 60, 70])
print(arr[1:4:1])
```

Output:

```
>>> [20 30 40]
```

For a 3D dimension, look at this example. Here the third element is [110,120,130,140,150] and 0:4 is the first element to the fourth one.

Example:

```
import numpy as np
myarr = np.array([[10, 20, 30, 40, 50], [60, 70, 80,
90, 10], [110, 120, 130, 140, 150]])
print(myarr[2, 0:4])
```

Output:

```
>>> [110 120 130 140]
```

The first part shows that the first element to the third one should be processed, and the slice is from the second element to the third one.

Example:

```
import numpy as np
myarr = np.array([[10, 20, 30, 40, 50], [60, 70, 80,
90, 100], [110, 120, 130, 140, 150]])
print(myarr[0:3, 1:3])
```

Output:

```
>>> [[20  30] [70  80] [120 130]]
```

2.2.5 Data Type

Here are the datatypes in NumPy:

TABLE 2.8   Data Types in NumPy

Symbol	Type
i	integer
b	boolean
u	unsigned integer
f	float
c	complex float
m	timedelta
M	datetime
O	object
S	string
U	unicode string
V	fixed chunk of memory for other type (void)

2.2.6 Array Data Check

You can use copy, view, and base to copy the current values, copy the last values, and check each array's original data values.

Example:

```
import numpy as np
myarr = np.array([10, 20, 30, 40, 50, 60, 70])
x = myarr.copy()
arr[0]=7
y = arr.view()
print(x)
```

```
print(y)
print(x.base)
print(y.base)
```

Output:

```
[10 20 30 40 50 60 70]
[7 20 30 40 50 60 70]
None
[7 20 30 40 50 60 70]
```

2.2.7 Shape and Reshape Array

The shape gives you the array's dimension, and the reshaping to change the array dimension depends on the array's size.

Example:

```
import numpy as np
myarr = np.array([11, 12, 13, 14, 15, 16, 17, 18,
90, 100, 110, 120, 130, 140])
print(myarr.shape)
newarr1 = myarr.reshape(2, 7, 1)
newarr2 = myarr.reshape(1, 7, 2)
print(newarr1)
print(newarr2)
```

Output:

```
(14,)
[[[11] [12] [13] [14] [15] [16] [17]] [[18] [90]
[100] [110] [120] [130] [140]]]
[[[11 12] [13 14] [15 16] [17 18]   [90 100][110 120] [130
140]]]
```

2.2.8 Array Iterating

Each dimension is presented by a for loop.

Example:

```
import numpy as np
myarr = np.array([[[10, 20, 30, 40], [50, 60, 70,
80]], [[90, 100, 110, 120], [130, 140, 150, 160]]])
```

```
for x in arr:
  for y in x:
    for z in y:
      print(z)
```

Output:

11,12,13,14,15,16,17,80,90,100,110,120,130,140,150,160

Example:

```
nditer() does the same things.
import numpy as np
myarr = np.array([[[10, 20, 30, 40], [50, 60, 70,
80]], [[90, 100, 110, 120], [130, 140, 150, 160]]])
for x in np.nditer(myarr):
  print(x)
```

Output:

11,12,13,14,15,16,17,80,90,100,110,120,130,140,150,160

2.2.9 Joining Array

For joining array, some methods like concatenate, stack, joining array and hstack, stacking along a row, vstack for stacking, columns and dstack for joining along with the height.

Example:

```
import numpy as np
arr1 = np.array([1, 2, 3])
arr2 = np.array([4, 5, 6])
arrn1 = np.concatenate((arr1, arr2))
arrn2 = np.stack((arr1, arr2), axis=1)
arrn3 = np.hstack((arr1, arr2))
arrn4 = np.vstack((arr1, arr2))
arrn5 = np.dstack((arr1, arr2))
print(arrn1)
print(arrn2)
print(arrn3)
print(arrn4)
print(arrn5)
```

Output:

```
[1 2 3 4]
[[1 3] [2 4]]
[1 2 3 4]
[[1 2] [3 4]]
[[[1 3] [2 4]]]
```

2.2.10 Splitting Array

Here array_split splits the array into **n** parts.

Example:

```
import numpy as np
myarr = np.array([[10, 20], [30, 40], [50, 60], [70,
80], [90, 100], [110, 120],[130, 140]])
newarr = np.array_split(myarr, 2)
print(newarr)
it splits the array to two parts (n=2).
```

Output:

```
[array([[10, 20],[30, 40],[50, 60],[70, 80]]),
array([[90, 100],[110, 120],[130, 140]])]
```

2.2.11 Searching Arrays

where () is used to find the index of the elements in the array.

Example:

```
import numpy as np
myarr = np.array([10, 20, 30, 40, 50, 60, 70, 20,
40, 50, 70])
x = np.where(myarr == 70)
print(x)
```

Output:

```
(array([6, 10], dtype=int64),)
```

2.2.12 Sorting Arrays

sort () put the elements in the array in the ordered sequence.

Example:

```
import numpy as np
arr1 = np.array([3, 2, 0, 1])
arr2 = np.array([[3, 2, 4], [5, 0, 1]])
arr3 = np.array(['banana', 'cherry', 'apple'])
print(np.sort(arr1))
print(np.sort(arr2))
print(np.sort(arr3))
```

Output:

```
[0 1 2 3]
[[2 3 4] [0 1 5]]
['apple' 'banana' 'cherry']
```

2.2.13 Filter Array

The array elements are filtered using boolean indexing.

Example:

```
import numpy as np
arr = np.array([1, 2, 3, 4])
x = [True, False, False, True]
newarr = arr[x]
print(newarr)
```

Output:

```
[1 4]
```

2.2.14 Random Numbers

There is a random module that has some methods like **randint()**, **rand()**, and **choice()**. **randint()** and **rand()** are used to create random numbers in a range, and **choice()** is used to choose an array element randomly.

Example:

```
from numpy import random
x1= random.rand()
x2= random.rand(2)
x3= random.rand(1, 2)
```

```
x4= random.randint(2)
x5= random.rand(1, 2)
x6=random.randint(10, size=(5))
x7 = random.choice([1,2,3,4,5,6,7,9], size=(1,2))
print(x1)
print(x2)
print(x3)
print(x4)
print(x5)
print(x6)
print(x7)
```

Output:

```
0.9991215682671595
[0.29059623 0.67536595]
[[0.69502737 0.99873108]]
0
[[0.27185965 0.13683672]]
[8 5 9 0 4]
[[1 3]]
```

2.2.15 Array Vectorization

Convert data to the vector-based operation, for example, for adding; look at these examples for adding **x** and **y**. Both give you the same results, but using the NumPy makes the computation faster and easier.

Example:

```
import numpy as np
x = [1, 2, 3, 4]
y = [5, 6, 7, 8]
z = []
t = np.add(x, y)
for i, j in zip(x, y):
   z.append(i + j)
print(t)
print(z)
```

Output:

```
[6 8 10 12]
[6, 8, 10, 12]
```

2.2.16 np.zeros and np.ones

It helps to create zero and one matrix.

These are the syntaxes:

```
numpy.zeros(shape, dtype=int, order='C')
numpy.ones(shape, dtype=int, order='C')
```

Example:

```
np.zeros((2, 2))
np.ones((2, 2))
```

2.2.17 hstack and vstack

These two functions append data horizontally and vertically.

Example:

```
a = np.array([1, 2, 3])
b = np.array([4, 5, 6])
print('Horizontally:', np.hstack((a, b)))
print('Vertically:', np.vstack((a, b)))
```

2.2.18 Generate Random Numbers

This is the syntax for generating random numbers:

```
numpy.random.normal(loc, scale, size)
```

that the parameters are:

loc: the mean

scale: standard deviation

size: number of returns

Example:

```
normal_array = np.random.normal(1, 0.7, 5)
print(normal _ array)
```

Output:

```
[1.35834557 0.17359591 1.35380164 0.65828157 0.10857762]
```

2.2.19 Mathematical Functions

It supports most statistical methods as follows:

TABLE 2.9   Statistical Methods

Function	Numpy
Min	np.min()
Max	np.max()
Mean	op.mean()
Median	op.median()
Standard deviation	np.stdt()

2.2.20 Dot Product and Matrix Multiplication

It computes the dot product using np.dot and np.matmul for matrix multiplication.

2.2.21 Determinant

You can use np.linalg.det to find the determinant of a matrix.

## CHAPTER 3

TensorFlow and Keras Fundamentals

3.1 HOW DOES TENSORFLOW WORK?

Google created TensorFlow in Google Brain. TensorFlow is a numerical computations framework for machine learning algorithms, especially deep neural networks. Many people like researchers, programmers, and data scientists use it in their projects. TensorFlow is compatible with several operating systems like Linux, macOS, and Windows, and it can run over desktops, clouds (as a web server like AWS and google cloud), and mobile (iOS or Android). Table 3.1 shows the comparisons between TensorFlow and the other frameworks.

There are two versions (1 and 2) for TensorFlow. The computation in TensorFlow is in a dataflow graph format, and in each graph, some operations like addition, represented by nodes and edges, define the data. The tensors (multi-dimensional data) go through a flow of operations and end in the next node. Tensor board is a toolkit for TensorFlow that helps us to follow the TensorFlow process visually. TensorFlow is designed based on graph computation and has several libraries that work with different APIs and are available for all developers (you can check TensorFlow's popularity on GitHub!). These features make TensorFlow one of the most interesting platforms for designing deep learning algorithms. It runs on CPU and

DOI: 10.1201/9781003025818-3

TABLE 3.1   Most Popular Deep Learning Frameworks

Library	Platform	Written in	Parallel Execution	Trained Models	CNN	RNN
Torch	Linux, macOS, Windows	Lua	Yes	Yes	Yes	Yes
Kears	Linux, macOS, Windows	Python	Yes	Yes	Yes	Yes
Theano	Cross-platform	Python	Yes	Yes	Yes	Yes
TensorFlow	Linux, macOS, Windows, Android	C++, Python, CUDA	Yes	Yes	Yes	Yes
Microsoft Cognitive Toolkit	Linux, Windows, macOS with Docker	C++	Yes	Yes	Yes	Yes
Caffe	Linux, macOS, Windows	C++	Yes	Yes	Yes	Yes
MXNet	Linux, macOS, Windows, Android, ios, JavaScript	C++	Yes	Yes	Yes	Yes

GPU on different single or multiple machines. Modeling using TensorFlow works in three main steps:

1. data preprocessing,

2. building a model, and

3. training and testing the model.

There are two types of tensor: (1) Constant and (2) Variable, and Tensor has some features like:

Dimension is the value that shows the structure of a tensor.

Figure 3.1 shows three examples of dimensions.

Rank is the number of directions in tensor. It is zero for a scaler number (for a vector, it depends on the dimensions). For example, in Figure 3.1, for 1D, the rank is 1. 2D, the rank is 2. 3D, the rank is 3, and so on.

Shape is the number of values in each dimension. The leaf in each graph contains the actual tensor. For example, the shape of the tensors in Figure 3.1 is:

3D: (4,5,4)

2D: (4,4)

1D: 4

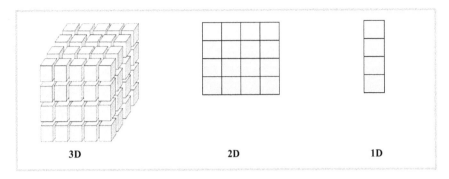

FIGURE 3.1   Three examples for three tensors dimensions.

Size is the total number of items in the tensor, and it is the product shape vector, for example, in Figure 3.1: 3D: 4*5*4=80, 2D: 4*4=16, and 1D: 4

3.2 TENSORS

Tensor is the base of the TensorFlow and is a vector of an n-dimensional matrix. It is used to show data. A tensor has three main properties:

1. unique label (name),

2. dimension (shape), and

3. datatype (dtype).

And there are three types of tensors that we can create:

1. tf.Variable: defining the variable,

2. tf.constant: defining the constant, and

3. tf.SparseTensor: defining the sparse tensor.

There are nodes and edges in TensorFlow that edges transfer the scaled values from the nodes in the current level to the nodes in the next level. Look at this example:

$$K = (3x + y)/y + 7$$

Figure 3.2 shows a computational graph for **K**. In this example, the **x** in the lowest level (leaf) is multiplied by **3**, and **y** is multiplied by **1**, then we

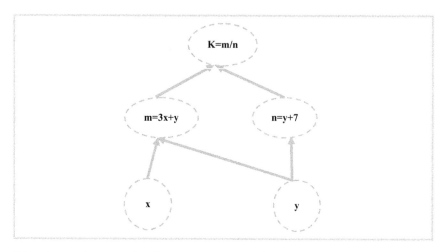

FIGURE 3.2   An example of a computation graph.

add them up in the new node in the next level. The current values of the node are assigned to **m**. Also, for another node, the **y** is added up by **7**, and the value will be assigned to **n**. The new node values will be transferred to the next node at the next level with a new operation. (The first step in TensorFlow is defining a tensor.)

Let's learn it more with some examples. For a float **0D** tensor (scalar):

Example:

```
r0_tensor = tf.constant(7)
print(r0 _ tensor)
```

Output:

```
tf.Tensor(7, shape=(), dtype=int32)
```

Let's make a float **1D** tensor:

Example:

```
r1_tensor = tf.constant([1.0, 2.0, 3.0])
print(r1 _ tensor)
```

Output:

```
tf.Tensor([1. 2. 3.], shape=(3,), dtype=float32)
```

Let's make a **2D** tensor:

Example:

```
rank_2_tensor = tf.constant([[1, 2],[3, 4],[5, 6]],
dtype=tf.float16)
print(rank _ 2 _ tensor)
```

Output:

```
tf.Tensor([[1. 2.][3. 4.] [5. 6.]], shape=(3, 2),
dtype=float16)
```

Let's make a **3D** tensor:

Example:

```
r3_tensor = tf.constant([[[1, 2, 3, 4, 5],[6, 7,
8, 9, 10]],[[11, 12, 13, 14, 15],[16, 17, 18, 19,
20]],[[21, 22, 23, 24, 25],[26, 27, 28, 29, 30]],])
print(r3 _ tensor)
```

Output:

```
tf.Tensor([[[ 1 2  3  4  5] [6  7  8  9 10]]  [[11
12 13 14 15] [16 17 18 19 20]] [[21 22 23 24 25]
 [26 27 28 29 30]]], shape=(3, 2, 5), dtype=int32)
```

Let's find the shape, size, and dimension of the matrix using TensorFlow:

Example:

```
r3D_tensor = tf.zeros([4, 5, 4])
print("Type of every element:", r3D_tensor.dtype)
print("Number of dimensions:", r3D_tensor.ndim)
print("Shape of tensor:", r3D_tensor.shape)
print("Elements along axis 0 of tensor:", r3D_
tensor.shape[0])
print("Elements along the last axis of tensor:",
r3D_tensor.shape[-1])
print("Total number of elements (4*4*5): ",
tf.size(r3D _ tensor).numpy())
```

Output:

```
Type of every element: <dtype: 'float32'>
Number of dimensions: 3
Shape of tensor: (4, 5, 4)
Elements along axis 0 of tensor: 4
Elements along the last axis of tensor: 4
Total number of elements (4*4*5):   80
```

3.3 TENSORFLOW

There are three main steps when you are using TensorFlow:

1. variable definition,

2. computation definition, and

3. operation execution.

Let's learn them better with some examples.

Step 1: define the variable

Example:

```
X1 = tf.constant([1, 3, 5])
X2 = tf.constant([2, 4, 6])
```

Step 2: define the computation

Example:

```
multiply= tf.multiply(X1, X2)
```

Step 3: print results

Example:

```
print(multiply)
```

Output:

```
tf.Tensor([2 12 30], shape=(3,), dtype=int32)
```

Example:

```
a = tf.constant([[2, 5],[1, 4]])
```

```
b = tf.constant([[1, 1],[1, 1]])
print(tf.add(a, b), "\n")
print(tf.multiply(a, b), "\n")
print(tf.matmul(a, b), "\n")
```

Output:

```
tf.Tensor([[3 6][2 5]], shape=(2, 2), dtype=int32)
tf.Tensor([[2 5][1 4]], shape=(2, 2), dtype=int32)
tf.Tensor ([[7 7][5 5]],   shape=(2, 2),   dtype=int32)
```

Example:

```
a = tf.constant([[12, 10],[2.,10.]])
x = tf.constant([[1.,0.],[0.,1.]])
b = tf.Variable(2.)
y = tf.matmul(a, x) + b
print(y.numpy())
```

Output:

```
[[14. 12.] [4. 12.]]
```

3.4 BUILDING AN NN USING TENSORFLOW

Here is an example of the Fashion-MNIST dataset by Zalando (Figure 3.3). It contains 70,000 images in 10 different categories with 28×28 images of clothing. The steps for creating a neural network structure are as follows:

Step 1: import the data,

Step 2: preprocessing the data,

Step 3: normalize the data,

Step 4: build the model, and

Step 5: train and evaluate the model.

3.4.1 Import the Data

In the first step, import the libraries and dataset from scikitlearn.

```
from __future__ import absolute_import, division,
print_function, unicode_literals
import numpy as np
```

```
import tensorflow as tf
from tensorflow import keras as ks
```

3.4.2 Load and Normalize the Data

Now, load the dataset and normalize the data for better training. The normalization of the data helps to better computation and less computation costs. It also can increase the accuracy of the results.

```
from sklearn.preprocessing import MinMaxScaler
(training_images, training_labels), (test_images,
  test_labels) = ks.datasets.fashion_mnist.load_
  data()y_train   = y_train.astype(int)
test_labels   = test_labels.astype(int)
batch_size =len(training_images)
scaler= MinMaxScaler()
training_images = scaler.fit_transform(training_
  images.astype(np.float64))
test_images = scaler.fit_transform(test_images.
  astype(np.float64))
print('Training Images Dataset Shape: {}'.
  format(training_images.shape))
print('No. of Training Images Dataset Labels: {}'.
  format(len(training_labels)))
print('Test Images Dataset Shape: {}'.format(test_
  images.shape))
print('No. of Test Images Dataset Labels: {}'.
  format(len(test_labels)))
training_images = training_images / 255.0
test _ images = test _ images / 255.0
```

Output:

```
Training Images Dataset Shape: (60000, 28, 28)
No. of Training Images Dataset Labels: 60000
Test Images Dataset Shape: (10000, 28, 28)
No. of Test Images Dataset Labels: 10000
```

3.4.3 Build the Model

You can define the model by determining the parameters and hyperparameters. These parameters are activation function, data shape, and the layers. Here we set the data shape to the 28*28 and the hidden and output activation functions are ReLU and softmax.

```
input_data_shape = (28, 28)
hidden_activation_function = 'relu'
output_activation_function = 'softmax'
nn_model = ks.models.Sequential()
nn_model.add(ks.layers.Flatten(input_shape=input_
data_shape, name='Input_layer'))
nn_model.add(ks.layers.Dense(32, activation=hidden_
activation_function, name='Hidden_layer'))
nn_model.add(ks.layers.Dense(10, activation=output_
activation_function, name='Output_layer'))
nn _ model.summary()
```

Output:

```
Layer (type)              Output Shape        Param #
=====================================================
Input_layer (Flatten)     (None, 784)         0
Hidden_layer (Dense)      (None, 64)          50240
Output_layer (Dense)      (None, 10)          650
=====================================================
Total params: 50, 890
Trainable params: 50, 890
Non-trainable params: 0
```

3.4.4 Train and Evaluate the Model

In the next step, you should train and evaluate the model. The optimizer here is ADAM (you can use another optimizer).

Step 1: Training

Train the model using the training data and the defined model.

```
optimizer = 'adam'
loss_function = 'sparse_categorical_crossentropy'
metric = ['accuracy']
nn_model.compile(optimizer=optimizer,
loss=loss_function,metrics=metric)
nn _ model.fit(training _ images, training _ labels,
epochs=20)
```

Output:

```
....
1875/1875 [===========] - 2s 967us/step - loss:
                          0.1831 - accuracy: 0.9317
Epoch 19/20
1875/1875 [===========] - 2s 1ms/step - loss: 0.1779
                          - accuracy: 0.9339
Epoch 20/20
1875/1875 [===========] - 2s 978us/step - loss:
                          0.1765 - accuracy: 0.9345
...
```

Step 2: Evaluation

Evaluate model using a part of the original data as evaluation data that give us some estimates about the model before testing and using with real-world problems:

```
training_loss, training_accuracy = nn_model.
  evaluate(training_images, training_labels)
print ('Training Data Accuracy {}'.
  format(round(float(training _ accuracy),2)))
```

Output:

```
1875/1875 [============] - 1s 639us/step - loss:
                          0.1694 - accuracy: 0.9378
Training Data Accuracy 0.94
```

Step 3: Testing

Test model using testing data:

```
test_loss, test_accuracy = nn_model.
evaluate(test_images,test_labels)
print('Test Data Accuracy {}'.
format(round(float(test _ accuracy),2)))
```

Output:

```
313/313 [==============] - 0s 1ms/step - loss:
                          0.3833 - accuracy: 0.8824
Test Data Accuracy 0.88
```

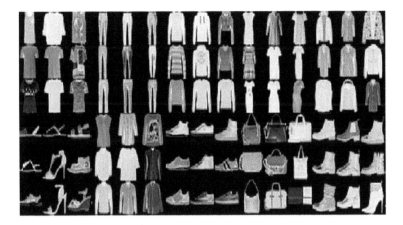

FIGURE 3.3   Fashion-MNIST data.

3.5 BUILDING A CNN USING TENSORFLOW

Here are the steps of creating a CNN using TensorFlow:

Step 1: upload data,

Step 2: input layer,

Step 3: convolutional layer and pooling layer,

Step 4: dense layer, and

Step 5: train and test the model.

3.5.1 Dataset

Upload the data at the first step. We are using the dataset in the previous example (Fashion-MNIST).

3.5.2 Input Layer

Define the parameter of the input layer like activation function and data shape. You should design these parts before start coding.

```
#define the input layer parameters
input_data_shape = (28, 28)
hidden_activation_function = 'relu'
```

```
output_activation_function = 'softmax'
dnn_model = ks.models.Sequential()
dnn _ model.summary()
```

3.5.3 Convolutional and Pooling Layers

Define and determine the convolution and pooling layer parameters. These parameters are the size of the pooling window or the inputs of the hidden layers and the number of the hidden layers.

```
dnn_model.add(ks.layers.Flatten(input_shape=input_
data_shape, name='Input_layer'))
dnn_model.add(ks.layers.Dense(256, activation=hidden_
activation_function, name='Hidden_layer_1'))
#     first Layer
pool1 = tf.compat.v1.layers.max_
pooling2d(inputs=conv1, pool_size=[2, 2], strides=2)
dnn_model.add(ks.layers.Dense(192, activation=hidden_
activation_function, name='Hidden_layer_2'))
#     Second Layer
pool2 = tf. compat.v1.layers.max_
pooling2d(inputs=conv2, pool_size=[2, 2], strides=2)
dnn _ model.add(ks.layers.Dense(128, activation=hidden _
activation _ function, name='Hidden _ layer _ 3'))
```

3.5.4 Dense Layer

Define the output layer parameters.

```
dnn _ model.add(ks.layers.Dense(10, activation=output _
activation _ function, name='Output _ layer'))
```

Now you can see the model summary.

```
dnn _ model.summary()
```

Output:

Layer (type)	Output Shape	Param #
Input_layer (Flatten)	(None, 784)	0
Hidden_layer_1 (Dense)	(None, 256)	200960
Hidden_layer_2 (Dense)	(None, 192)	49344
Hidden_layer_3 (Dense)	(None, 128)	24704
Output_layer (Dense)	(None, 10)	1290

```
Total params: 276, 298
Trainable params: 276, 298
Non-trainable params: 0
```

3.5.5 Train and Evaluate the Model

Now do the prediction and evaluation on training data:

```
training_loss, training_accuracy = dnn_model.
evaluate(training_images, training_labels)
print('Training Data Accuracy {}'.
format(round(float(training _ accuracy),2)))
```

Output:

```
1875/1875 [==========] - 2s 1ms/step - loss: 0.1607
                         - accuracy: 0.9387
Training Data Accuracy 0.94
```

3.5.6 Test the Model

Then in the last part do the test on the test data:

```
test_loss, test_accuracy = dnn_model.evaluate(test_
images, test_labels)
print('Test Data Accuracy {}'.
format(round(float(test _ accuracy),2)))
```

Output:

```
313/313 [==============================] - 0s 2ms/
step - loss: 0.3824 - accuracy: 0.8921
Test Data Accuracy 0.89
```

3.6 SETUP AND INSTALL KERAS

Keras is one of the easy platforms to use python libraries and is on top of some machine learning platforms like TensorFlow to create deep learning models. The CNN and RNN models are easy to use and quick to implement. TensorFlow provides both low- and high-level APIs, and Keras provides the low level. It also helps to reduce the computation costs. Here, we review some fundamentals and main concepts of the Keras and explain them with some examples. You also can use the Keras website (https://keras.io/) for more details and examples. There are some requirements to start using Keras as follows:

1. Python 3.5 or higher

2. SciPy with NumPy

3. TensorFlow

4. Any OS (Windows, Linux, or Mac)

3.6.1 Create a Virtual Environment

Creating a virtual environment helps you to set up different installed packages for different projects separately. For example, you can install it on python3:

```
python3 -m venv kerasenv
```

3.6.2 Activate the Environment

After creating the virtual environment, you should activate it if you like to use it.

- Linux/Mac

```
$ cd kerasvenv kerasvenv $ source bin/activate
```

- Windows

```
.\env\Scripts\activate
```

3.6.3 Python Libraries

You may need these python dependencies in your project to install them by using **pip** or **pip3**. Here we review some of these requirements with examples to install Keras and use it and its libraries.

- **Numpy**

```
pip install numpy
```

- **Pandas**

```
pip install pandas
```

- **Scikit-learn**

```
pip install -U scikit-learn
```

- **Matplotlib**

```
pip install matplotlib
```

- **Scipy**

```
pip install scipy
```

- **Seaborn**

```
pip pip install seaborninstall -U scikit-learn
```

Now you can install Keras

```
pip install keras
```

If TensorFlow is not installed on your system, please install it.

```
pip install TensorFlow
```

after finishing all parts of your project, you can quit the environment.

```
deactivate
```

Please check your python version and its requirements for using pip or pip3. Creating, activating, and deactivating the virtual environment helps you organize your codes and modules for different projects.

3.6.4 Available Modules

These are available modules in Keras that you should learn to use and set when you plan to create a model with Keras:

Regularizes: A list of regularizers.

Constraints: A list of constraints.

Activations: A list of activator functions.

Losses: A list of the loss functions.

Metrics: A list of metrics functions.

Optimizers: A list of optimizer functions.

Callback: A list of the callback functions.

Text processing: functions to convert text into NumPy array.

Image processing: functions to convert images into NumPy.

Sequence processing: functions to generate time-based data from the given input data.

Backend: function of the backend library like TensorFlow.

Utilities: many utility functions are useful in deep learning.

3.6.5 Import Libraries and Modules

Here are some of the libraries and modules and the commands for importing. Please try these codes on your computer.

- **NumPy**

```
Import numpy as np
```

- **Keras model module**

```
from keras.models import Sequential
```

- **Keras core layers**

```
from keras.layers import Dense, Dropout, Activation, Flatten
```

- **Keras CNN Layers**

```
from keras.layers import Convoluton2D, MaxPooling2D
```

- **Utilities**

```
from keras.utils import np_utils
```

These are the most important libraries that we almost use in all our projects when we are using Keras.

3.6.6 Train and Predict the Model

After importing the libraries, we should train the model and test it. Here are some modules in Keras that we can use.

- **Compile**:

It is used to configure the learning model

Example:

```
compile(
    optimizer,
    loss = None,
    metrics = None,
    loss_weights = None,
    sample_weight_mode = None,
    weighted_metrics = None,
    target_tensors = None
)
model.compile(loss = 'mean_squared_error', optimizer
= 'sgd', metrics = [metrics.categorical_accuracy])
```

- **Fit**:

Use **fit** to train the model using training data.

Example:

```
model.fit(X, y, epochs = , batch_size = )
```

where:

X, y – It is a tuple to evaluate your data.

epochs – no of times the model is needed to be evaluated during training.

batch_size – training instances.

- **Evaluate**:

Use it to do evaluation using evaluation or test data. It is a module of the model, and its main inputs are the input data and their labels.

Example:

```
score = model.evaluate(x _ test, y _ test, verbose = 0)
```

- **Predict**:

use it to predict and test the model for new input.

Example:

```
predict (
    x,
    batch_size = None,
    verbose = 0,
    steps = None,
    callbacks = None,
    max_queue_size = 10,
    workers = 1,
    use_multiprocessing = False
)
```

3.7 IMPLEMENT AN EXAMPLE USING KERAS

The Keras API has three main parts:

- **Model**: There are two main sequential models to implement the simple model and function or implementing the complex model.

- **Layer**: There are some layers like convolution, pooling, and recurrent layers.

- **Modules**: Some modules like the activation function provide functions like softmax and ReLU; loss function that provides functions like MSE; optimizer that provides functions like adam and sgd; and regularizer that provides functions like L_1 and L_2.

3.7.1 MNIST Example

There are eight main steps that we explain them with code example on MNIST dataset data.

Step 1 – Import the Modules

In the first step, you should import the modules you need for implementation.

```
import keras
from keras.datasets import mnist
from keras.models import Sequential
from keras.layers import Dense, Dropout, Flatten
from keras.layers import Conv2D, MaxPooling2D
from keras import backend as K
import numpy as np
```

Step 2 – Load Data

Determine your dataset and load the data in the second step.

```
(x _ train, y _ train), (x _ test, y _ test) = mnist.
load _ data()
```

Step 3 – Process the Data

Before using the data, you can do some process on the data that helps to achieve better results.

```
img_rows, img_cols = 28, 28
if K.image_data_format() == 'channels_first':
   x_train = x_train.reshape(x_train.shape[0], 1,
img_rows, img_cols)
   x_test = x_test.reshape(x_test.shape[0], 1, img_
rows, img_cols)
   input_shape = (1, img_rows, img_cols)
```

```
else:
   x_train = x_train.reshape(x_train.shape[0], img_
rows, img_cols, 1)
x_test = x_test.reshape(x_test.shape[0], img_rows,
img_cols, 1)
input_shape = (img_rows, img_cols, 1)
x_train = x_train.astype('float32')
x_test = x_test.astype('float32')
x_train /= 255
x_test /= 255
y_train = keras.utils.to_categorical(y_train, 10)
y _ test = keras.utils.to _ categorical(y _ test, 10)
```

Step 4 – Create the Model

You can define the model parameters and hyperparameters in this step.

```
model = Sequential()
model.add(Conv2D(32, kernel_size = (3, 3),
activation = 'relu', input_shape = input_shape))
model.add(Conv2D(64, (3, 3), activation = 'relu'))
model.add(MaxPooling2D(pool_size = (2, 2)))
model.add(Dropout(0.25)) model.add(Flatten())
model.add(Dense(128, activation = 'relu'))
model.add(Dropout(0.5))
model.add(Dense(10, activation = 'softmax'))
```

Step 5 – Compile the Model

Define the loss function, optimizer, and metric to compile and prepare the model for training.

```
model.compile(loss = keras.losses.categorical _
crossentropy, optimizer = keras.optimizers.Adadelta(),
metrics = ['accuracy'])
```

Step 6 – Train the Model

Train the model using training data.

```
model.fit(
   x_train, y_train,
   batch_size = 128,
   epochs = 12,
```

```
    verbose = 1,
    validation_data = (x_test, y_test)
)
```

Step 7 – Evaluate the Model

Evaluate the trained model using evaluation data to check the model.

```
score = model.evaluate(x_test, y_test, verbose = 0)
print('Test loss:', score[0])
print('Test accuracy:', score[1])
```

Step 8 – Test the Model

Test the evaluated model using test data before using the model for real-world problem and data.

```
pred = model.predict(x_test)
pred = np.argmax(pred, axis = 1)[:5]
label = np.argmax(y_test,axis = 1)[:5]
print(pred)
print(label)
```

## CHAPTER 4

Artificial Neural Networks (ANNs) Fundamentals and Architectures

4.1 TERMINOLOGY

Here, we review some terminologies that we use in Chapters 4-8.

4.1.1 Inputs

The learning algorithms (here, NNs) use data for training the models. These data are input data, and usually, we show them as a vector of data sample with **x**. A set of **x** vectors gives us **X** as a matrix of inputs (**N**). Each vector sample **x** has **1…m** features that are the data values of each vector. For example, suppose we have **N=1000** apples, and each sample represents a vector of data **X**= [x_1=**price** x_2=**color** x_3=**shape**]. The **m** is the number of features in the vector data sample that its value is **3**.

4.1.2 Weights

The weights are the values that are updated by the learning algorithms to train the model. Usually, each $\mathbf{w}_{ij}$ is the vector weights between two nodes (**i** and **j**). The set of weights gives us a matrix that we show by **W**.

DOI: 10.1201/9781003025818-4

4.1.3 Outputs

The learning algorithms in the last step give us a set of data as outputs. We usually show these values using **y** as a vector of output values y_j, (j =1...k). For example, if the outputs are **0** (apple) and **1** (non-apple), the **y** dimension is **k=2**, and it is a binary classification problem.

4.1.4 Targets

These are the values that their dimension is the same as outputs (**k**), and we need them in the supervised learning algorithms. Moreover, they give us the correct values that the model should provide as outputs (target) values.

4.1.5 Activation Function

We use some mathematical functions to let the input of each layer pass (make output) and, after reaching a value more than a threshold, go to the next layer. We discuss in more detail this concept and its types.

4.1.6 Error

The error is the difference between the output value and the target. We show it with **E**, and the learning goal is to make it small by a limit or as much as possible.

4.1.7 Training, Testing, and Validation Sets

We divide the database data into three main categories: training data to teach the model, validation data to certify the model, and testing data to examine the model. We explain these three types in more detail later.

4.1.8 Overfitting

When we train the model, we should care about generalization. If we train the model a lot and make the model very complicated, there is a possibility that the model does not generalize well, and then it cannot fit the data correctly. We cannot use training data because we already used them to train the model. We also need testing data for testing the model (we can use validation data for this purpose).

4.1.9 Underfitting

Underfitting is another concept that is the opposite of overfitting, and it happens when a learning model cannot simulate the behavior and relationships between a dataset's values and the target variable (Figure 4.1).

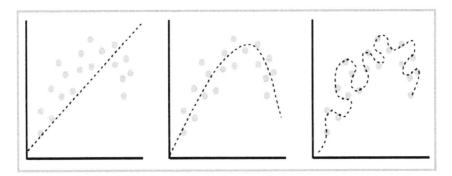

FIGURE 4.1   Underfitting(left), normal(middle), and overfitting(right).

4.1.10 Confusion Matrix

There are several methods for finding the accuracy of the algorithms. The confusion matrix is the method that we can use for classification problems. To find the confusion matrix, you can create a square matrix that, on the horizontal and vertical directions, we have both classes' values. We can assume the top of the table as predicted values and the left-hand side as the targets. For example, the values at the position **(i, j)** tell us the number of times the output predicted as class **j** when the target was **i**. Let me explain with an example (if we have two classes, then we have a 2×2 Table 4.1 as follows).

The value of t(1,1) =4 means four times that the output predicted as class C1 when the target was C1. For t(2,1) =2, when the output was predicted two times as class C1, the target was C2. Also, the value of t(1,2)=1 means one time that the output predicted as class C2 when the target was C1, and the last one for t(2,2)= 7, the output predicted seven times as class C2 when the target was C2. If you are looking for one number, you can sum the values leading diagonal and divide it by the sum of all values. For example, here the value is:

```
values leading diagonal= 4+7=11
whole values=4+1+2+7=14
```

TABLE 4.1   Confusion Matrix for Two Classes

Targets	Predicted Values	
	C1	C2
C1	4	1
C2	2	7

then we have:

```
11/14=.785
```

You can multiply this number by 100 and find a percentage:

```
.785×100=78.5 %
```

4.1.11 Accuracy Metrics

There are four definitions as accuracy metrics that you should know:

True positive (TP): the observation that is correctly classified (for example, to class 1). For instance, if the classification is based on the apple and not apple, if the object is apple and classified as apple, it is **TP**.

False positive (FP): the observation is not correctly classified (for example, to class 1). For instance, if the object is not apple and classified as apple, it is **FP**.

True negative (TN): the observation that correctly is not classified (for example, to class 1). For instance, if the object is not an apple and classified as not an apple, it is **TN**.

False negative (FN): the observation that mistake is not classified (for example, class 1). For instance, if the object is not apple and is classified as apple, it is **FN** (Table 4.2).

There are five definitions to find the accuracy based on these four values:

$$\text{Accuracy} = (\text{TP} + \text{FP}) / (\text{TP} + \text{FP} + \text{TN} + \text{FN})$$

$$\text{Sensitivity} = (\text{TP}) / (\text{TP} + \text{FN})$$

TABLE 4.2   Accuracy Metrics

		Actual	
		Positive	**Negative**
Predicted	Positive	TP	FP
	Negative	FN	TN

$$\text{Specificity} = \text{TN} / (\text{TN} + \text{FP})$$

$$\text{Precision} = \text{TP} / (\text{TP} + \text{FP})$$

$$\text{Recall} = \text{TP} / (\text{TP} + \text{FN})$$

Each of these values shows different aspects of model accuracy.

4.1.12 Balanced and Unbalanced Datasets

The dataset is balanced if the positive and negative examples have the same number in the dataset. We usually assumed that the dataset is balanced, but in the real-world dataset, they are not balanced (unbalanced datasets). For finding the accuracy in the balanced dataset, we can calculate and use this value:

$$\textbf{Accuracy} = (\text{Sensitivity} + \text{Specificity}) / 2$$

Also, there is another measurement based on those four values that its name is **MCC** (Matthew's Correlation Coefficient) and is calculated as follows:

$$\begin{aligned} \text{MCC} = ((\text{TP} \times \text{TN}) - (\text{FP} \times \text{FN})) / (\sqrt{(\text{TP} + \text{FP}) \times (\text{TP} + \text{FN})} \\ \times (\text{TN} + \text{FP}) \times (\text{TN} + \text{FN})) \end{aligned}$$

4.1.13 One Hot Encoding

Suppose there are categorical features in the dataset (for example, color), and there are three main channels for colors (**R=Red, G=Green,** and **B= Blue**)). Then, you can encode these string values to the numbers for using these data in the machine learning algorithm. Let's do this example:

Red --> 0

Green --> 1

Blue --> 2

These values are unique, and, in the data, if there are **k** features (here **k=3**), there are **k** unique numbers, and each feature is assigned to **One** unique value. Look at Table 4.3:

TABLE 4.3   Encoding RGB Values

Color Values	Red	Green	Blue
Green	0	1	0
Red	1	0	0
Blue	0	0	1
Red	1	0	0

```
The input is: {Green, Red, Blue, Red} and,
The output is: {(0,1,0), (1,0,0), (0,0,1), (1,0,0)}.
```

Please be careful that this method increases the dimensionality of the dataset. For example, in the previous example, the input dimension is 4×1, and the output is 4×3. When we are working with real data, it is possible that the input dimension is high, and then it makes the output dimension very high and then makes the computation high.

4.2 ARTIFICIAL NEURAL NETWORKS (ANNS)

ANNs were introduced by Warren McCulloch and Walter Pitts in 1943, who described a computational model of how biological neurons work in animal brains to perform computations. In the early 1980s, there were some interests in studying ANNs by researching and developing new algorithms and architectures. Along with these researches, some other powerful techniques, such as **Support Vector Machines (SVMs)**, were presented that showed better results in some experiments in comparison to the ANNs. Recently, developing a new generation of ANNs (deep learning) has made neural networks one of the hottest topics and tools for researchers, scientists, and engineers, and it seems ANNs and their developments and extensions will have more impact on the future of technology and human life. Here, in this chapter, the fundamentals of the ANNs and then some famous ANNs architectures with their formulation are presented.

4.2.1 Biological Neuron

The base elements of the human and animal neurological systems are neuron cells. They contain the nucleus (soma), many branches called dendrites, and one extended part called the axon. Neuron cells receive signals (short electrical impulses) from other neurons. For example, a neuron will fire (transmit) its signals when it receives enough threshold of signal

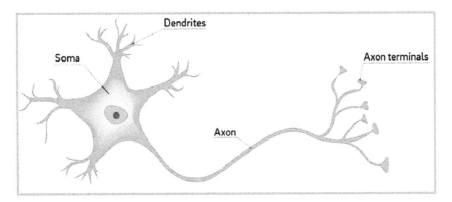

FIGURE 4.2   Biological neural cell.

strength. There are still many kinds of research in this field, trying to find the details of these biological network operations and functions (Figure 4.2).

4.2.2 Artificial Neuron

The artificial neuron is designed based on some basis of biological neuron cell structure and processes. Table 4.4 shows some of these bases and their similar components in ANNs. For example, neuron cells transfer signals through dendrites and axons, and in the ANNs, sample data are transferred through inputs and outputs. Also, soma decides when the signals can transfer to the axons, and the activation functions do a similar task in ANNs. The structure of neuron cells, such as shape, size, and structure, can define cells' capability and importance in networks for transferring the signals. It is simulated as weights in the ANNs, which define the importance of each neuron in the network.

Figure 4.3 shows an artificial neural cell structure whose main elements are inputs (data samples and weights) that are the impulse signals and the neuron structure, activation function (soma), and the output (the impulse input transfer to the next neuron through the dendrites).

TABLE 4.4   The Similarity Between Biological and Artificial Neurons

Biological Neuron	Artificial Neuron
Dendrites	Input connections
Soma	Activation function
Axons	Output connections
Neuron size and shapes, and features	Weights

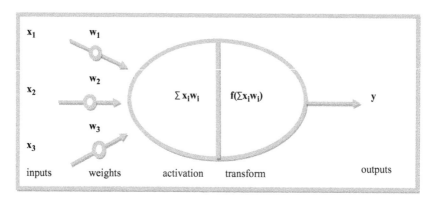

FIGURE 4.3   Artificial neuron element.

4.3 ACTIVATION FUNCTIONS

ANNs simulate linear and nonlinear behavioral models. They deploy activation functions for simulating nonlinear behaviors (most of the real-world problems are nonlinear). There are several activation functions, but the most popular ones are sigmoid (sig), hyperbolic tangent (tan), Rectifying Linear Unit (ReLU), leaky ReLU, and softmax. The question is, which one of them is the best? Some methods, such as cross-validation and some active research, help us find the best.

4.3.1 Sigmoid (sig)

The probability of everything has a value between 0 and 1. There are many models that their outputs are probability values. For these problems, a sigmoid can be the right choice. The sigmoid is also differentiable (its curve's slope can be calculated for every two points). Figure 4.4 Shows a sigmoid function.

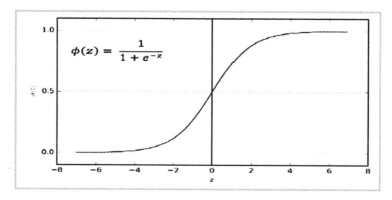

FIGURE 4.4   Sigmoid (sig) function.

4.3.2 Tanh or Hyperbolic Tangent (tan)

The value range of this activation function is [-1 to 1], and it maps the negative to the negative's values, and zero values will be near zero. Also, it is differentiable and is used mainly for classification problems. Figure 4.5 shows its shape.

4.3.3 Rectified Linear Unit (ReLU)

The ReLU value range is [0, infinity), and its output is zero when **z** is less than zero and is equal to **z** when **z** is above or equal to zero (**max** (0, x) and it deletes all negative values). Thus, it helps reduce the vanishing gradient problem, and on the other hand, the network that uses ReLU does not map the negative values appropriately. Because of removing the vanishing gradient problem and reducing the computation cost, it is an excellent choice to be used a lot in the deep learning algorithms. Figure 4.6 shows the ReLU shape, and as you can see, the values less than zero are zero, and the values greater than zero stays on a linear function.

$$R(z)=\textbf{max } (0, z)$$

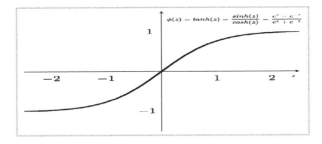

FIGURE 4.5   Hyperbolic tangent (tan) function.

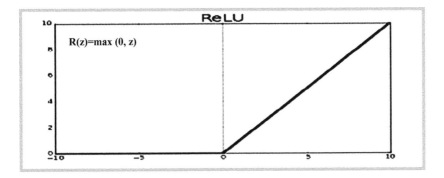

FIGURE 4.6   Rectifying Linear Unit (ReLU) function.

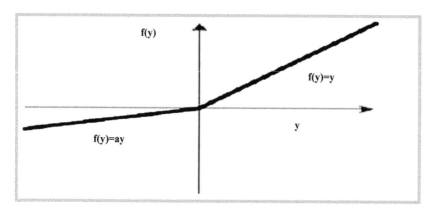

FIGURE 4.7   Leaky Rectifying Linear Unit (LReLU).

4.3.4 Leaky ReLU

The Leaky ReLU version of the ReLU function maps the negative values to some negative values and the positive values to the positive values. Its range is (-infinity to +infinity). Figure 4.7 Shows its shape.

4.3.5 Softmax

The softmax usually is utilized for the last layer or output layer. Its output is multiple, and it can cover the multiple class problems category. Figure 4.8 shows how softmax works.Softmax normalizes each class's output to the range between 0 and 1 (probability value dividing by sum).

$$S(y_i) = e^{y_i} \Big/ \sum_{j=1..n} e^{y_j}$$

The **S** is the softmax function, **y** is an input vector to the **S** and has **n** elements (like y_i that has a value between (-inf, +inf)) for **n** classes. **e** is the standard exponential function.

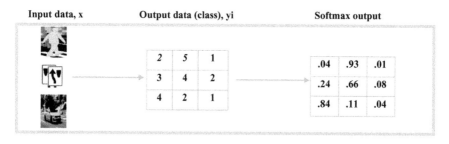

FIGURE 4.8   How softmax works!

4.4 LOSS FUNCTION

A loss function (cost function) is a function that shows how far is our predicted model from our desire model. It extracts by calculating the loss values (the difference between the predicted outputs and the desired (target)values). The several types of loss functions are in three main categories:

a) **Regressive loss functions**: such as **M**ean **S**quare **E**rror (MSE) and **A**bsolute **E**rror (AE),

b) **Classification loss functions**: such as **B**inary **C**ross-**E**ntropy (BCE), **N**egative **L**og-**L**ikelihood (NL), **S**oft **M**argin **C**lassifier (SMC), and

c) **Embedding loss functions**: such as **M**ean **A**bsolute **E**rror-MAE (L_1), **M**ean **S**quared **E**rror- MSE (L_2), and **C**osine **E**rror (CE).

The most popular ones are Cross-entropy Loss and Mean Squared Error-MSE (L_2) Loss.

4.4.1 Cross-Entropy Loss

It is a probability value and is the difference between predicted and actual costs. Figure 4.9 shows its graph.

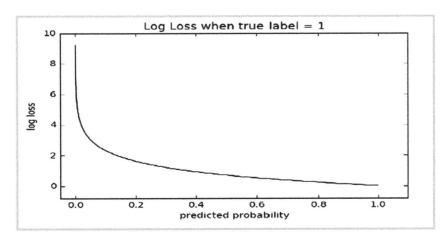

FIGURE 4.9   Cross-entropy loss graph.

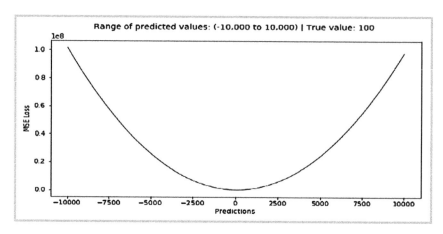

FIGURE 4.10   MSE (L_2) loss graph.

4.4.2 MSE (L_2) Loss

L2 is calculated by:

$$MSE = \frac{\sum\limits_{i=1}^{n}\left(y - y_i^p\right)^2}{n}$$

Figure 4.10 shows the L_2 graph representing an **MSE** function where the **MSE** loss reaches its minimum value at prediction = 100.

4.5 OPTIMIZATION FUNCTIONS

The three most popular optimization algorithms are **S**tochastic **G**radient **D**ecent (SGD), Adagrad, and Adam. Overall, the SGD is much faster than others. There is a tradeoff between speed and better results (accuracy). When data grows, the model becomes more complicated, and then choosing an optimization function is challenging. We should know two concepts before going to some famous optimization methods: learning rate and convex.

4.5.1 Learning Rate

Optimization algorithms update the network's weights and biases and have two categories: constant learning rate and adaptive learning rate. Learning rate is the step size value that optimization algorithms use it when the weights are training during the training stage. Its value is small and generally between 0.0 and 1.0, and choosing the improper value can affect the training convergence. Figure 4.11 shows some of these situations.

4.5.2 Convex

A function is called convex if we make a line between any two points on the graph, then it lies above or under the graph between the two points (Figure 4.12).

4.5.3 Gradient Descent

Gradient descent is one of the most popular optimization methods and gives the optimal value along the gradient descent direction. This method

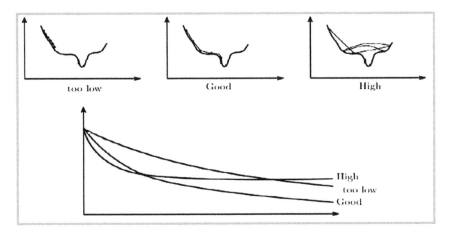

FIGURE 4.11   Different learning rate values.

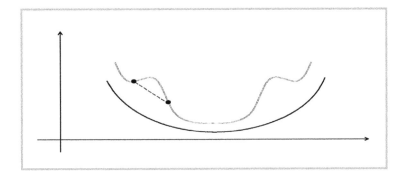

FIGURE 4.12   The top curve is non-convex, and the bottom one is convex.

is the most general and popular solution when the objective function is convex. One of its issues is the updating process in each step. When the gradient of all data is calculated, the GD's computation cost goes high, especially when the data size is very high. It also takes more time to converge when the data include more noise or biased data.

4.5.4 Stochastic Gradient Descent

Gradient Descent (GD) calculates gradient to find local minima, and Stochastic Gradient Descent (SGD) updates training example's parameter (SGD updates the parameters randomly). Its computation cost is efficient, and it is not necessarily dependent on the whole data. Its problem is choosing the proper learning rate. Maybe choosing one learning rate for all parameters is not the right solution, and it may fall at the saddle point.

4.5.5 Adagrad

Manually tuning the learning rate is not needed here because, for each parameter, it uses a different learning rate at a time based on the past gradients. In this method, the learning rate adjusts adaptively to the squares of all previous gradient values. With a more extensive learning rate, the learning speed is faster. The method is proper for sparse gradient problems. On the other hand, there is possibility that through time, all gradient values will be larger and maybe make the learning rate close to zero, and then the parameters do not update correctly. This method is not proper for a non-convex problem.

4.5.6 Adam

Adam stands for Adaptive Moment estimation and calculates different learning rates. This method is a combination of momentum and adaptive method. This method is proper for non-convex problems with a large amount of data and the high dimension of feature space. Most deep learning methods need large datasets, and then Adam can be one of the best fits for deep learning projects. One of its issues is the possibility of not being converge in some cases. Figure 4.13 shows the three methods' changes (GD, SGD, Adagrad, and Adam).

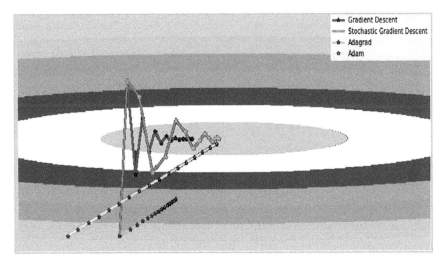

FIGURE 4.13   Four optimization function graphs.

4.6 LINEAR AND NONLINEAR FUNCTIONS

There are several input variables in the neural networks' formula like samples inputs **x**, weights **w**, and the **b**, as bias. By changing the values of these parameters, you can find different lines to separate the data. If you cannot separate the data linearly, you can use some functions to transfer data to the new space to make them linearly separable (these functions are known as the kernel).

4.6.1 Linear Function

Here, at first, we show the simplest version of the neural network for modeling linear functions:

$$f(x) = w \times x + b$$

x is input samples, **w** is the weight, and **b** is the bias. Figure 4.14 shows a graph of connection between these parts with vertices and edges simulation of neuron cells. The learning algorithm finds the best match for **(w, b)** to find the best approximation of the model that fits data **(x)** to the target **(f(x))**. The **x** is the matrix of input vectors that each vector includes the feature values of the data objects. For example, if the object is an apple,

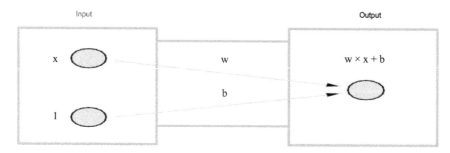

FIGURE 4.14   Vertices are neurons (data sample), and edges are weights and biases.

then the features are color, taste, and price (three values), and if we have seven different instants for apple, then the **x** size is 7×3= 21. 7 rows, that each row is representing an apple and each row has three columns that demonstrate the three selected features (Figure 4.14).

The value of **w** is initiated randomly, and the network training purpose is to find the best **w**, which gives us the best results (in the regression or classification problems).

When we choose the linear activation function, it does not work for the backpropagation because the derivative is constant, and it cannot help us update the weights in returning to the inputs and find the best weights. It does not work for nonlinear problems because the output is linear in any architecture (even with several neurons and layers). Therefore, it cannot simulate the nonlinear behavior of a problem. Figure 4.15 demonstrates the linear function that its derivative is constant and cannot simulate the nonlinear models.

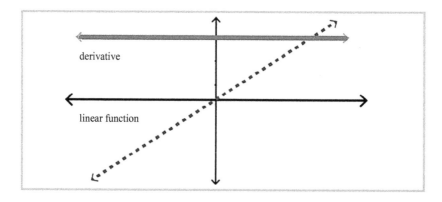

FIGURE 4.15   Linear function and its derivative.

4.6.2 Nonlinear Functions

In a real-world problem, there are some problems with nonlinearity in their behaviors. Deploying nonlinear functions (Activation Function (AF)) helps to simulate this type of model. We discussed some of them in the previous section. Here, we have one of the most popular ones in a neural network (the sigmoid function):

$$f(x) = sig(w \times x + b)$$

Figure 4.16 shows how to use sigmoid for nonlinearity simulation. It gives us a smooth gradient, besides its clear prediction (its values are limited between 0 and 1).

The nonlinear activation function covers two problems mentioned in the previous section to deploy in backpropagation and demonstrate the effect of more neurons and layers in the training process, especially in deep neural networks. However, its computation cost is high, and the gradients do not change in the high value of **x** (vanishing gradient problem). We can use the **ReLU** function that covers nonlinearity and is cost-efficient. Its problem is just about the negative value that the network cannot learn for these data. However, **Leaky ReLU** does not provide clear predictions for negative values; it solves this issue.

You can see the vanishing gradient problem in Figure 4.17 and the learning problem for negative values in Figure 4.18.

As you can see, it is also possible that **ReLU** includes some issues and problems, and maybe **leaky ReLU** solves them.

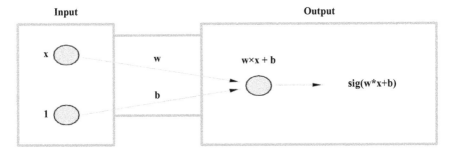

FIGURE 4.16   Using sigmoid for nonlinearity modeling.

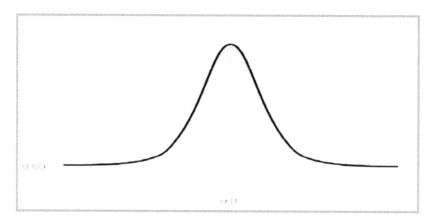

FIGURE 4.17   Derivatives for sigmoid.

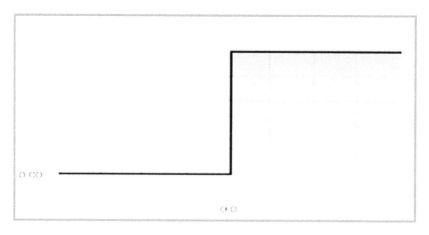

FIGURE 4.18   Derivatives for ReLU.

4.7 ANNS ARCHITECTURES

4.7.1 Feed Forward Neural Networks (FFNNs)

An FFNN is an artificial neural network without any form of a cycle in connections between nodes. It flows the information from one direction (input to the hidden layer and then output layer). FFNN is the simplest form of NNs that the information is processed only in one direction. Figure 4.18 shows the architecture of FFNN.

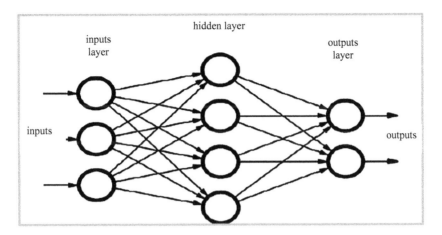

FIGURE 4.19   FFNN architecture.

FFNN is a simple network that has input, hidden, and output layers. The combination of neurons in each layer will forward propagate to the next layer. Then it goes to the activation function, and the outputs and their combinations are the inputs of the next layer, and it will continue for all layers, up to the last layer that gives the final outputs. For example, if the network has one input, one hidden, and one output layer as shown in Figure 4.19 and the **X** be the sample input vector, **X**= (x_1, x_2) and $\mathbf{W_h}=(w_{h11}, w_{h12}, w_{h21}, w_{h22})$ be the weights of the hidden layer and $\mathbf{Wo}=(w_{o11}, w_{o12}, w_{o13}, w_{o21}, w_{o22}, w_{o23}, w_{o31}, w_{o32}, w_{o33})$ be the weights of the output layer and **a** be the activation function then the prediction is equal to:

```
prediction=a(a(X*Wₕ)*Wₒ)
```

These are the steps:

Step 1: Calculate the weighted input to the hidden layer by multiplying **X** by hidden weight $\mathbf{W_h}$.

Step 2: Apply the activation function and pass the results to the next layer.

Step 3: Repeat steps 1 and 2 for all layers.

The algorithm uses the **X** data to calculate the combination of data **(X)** and weights **(W)** and bias **(b)** and applies activation function on it through all layers to get output. Two famous types of feedforwards networks are single- and multi-layer perceptron. The pseudo of the algorithm is:

```
Forward (x):
y₀=x
for l=1: L do:
        c₁=w₁ᵀy₁₋₁ + b₁
        y₁= a(c₁)
end
return (y₁)
```

4.7.1.1 FFN Example with TensorFlow

Step 1: Import Libraries

```
import tensorflow as tf
import numpy as np
from tensorflow import keras
```

Step 2: Load Data

```
from keras.datasets import mnist
(x _ train, y _ train), (x _ test, y _ test) = mnist.
load _ data()
```

Step 3: One Hot and Normalization Data

```
y_train = tf.one_hot(y_train, 10)
y_test = tf.one_hot(y_test, 10)
x_train = x_train / 255.0
x _ test = x _ test / 255.0
```

Step 4: Making Model

```
model = keras.Sequential([
    keras.layers.Flatten(input_shape=(28, 28)),
    keras.layers.Dense(256, activation='relu'),
    keras.layers.Dense(32, activation='relu'),
    keras.layers.Dense(10, activation='softmax')
])
```

Step 5: Model Summary

```
model.summary()
Model: "sequential"
```

Layer (type)	Output Shape	Param #
flatten_2 (Flatten)	(None, 784)	0
dense_6 (Dense)	(None, 256)	200960
dense_7 (Dense)	(None, 32)	8224
dense_8 (Dense)	(None, 10)	330

```
Total params: 209,514
Trainable params: 209,514
Non-trainable params: 0
```

Step 6: Compile the Model

```
model.compile(loss='categorical _ crossentropy',
metrics=['accuracy'], optimizer='adam')
```

Step 7: Train the Model

```
n_val = 5000
n_train = 60000
n_test = 10000
batch_size=100
epochs=100
steps_per_epoch = int((n_train-n_val)/batch_size)
n_val = 5000
validation_split = n_val/n_train
validation_steps = int(n_val / batch_size)
test_steps = int(n_test/batch_size)
history = model.fit(x_train, y_train, epochs=epochs,
steps_per_epoch=steps_per_epoch, validation_split=
validation_split, validation_steps=validation_steps,
callbacks=[tensorboard_callback])
```

Step 8: Test the Model

```
score = model.evaluate(x_test, y_test, steps=test_
steps, verbose=0)
```

```
print('Test loss:', score[0])
print('Test accuracy:', score[1])
```

4.7.2 Backpropagation

Backpropagation is a supervised learning algorithm, and it needs to be trained by training sample data. Here are the steps of implementing back-propagation algorithm:

Step 1: Forward Propagation: data vector **x** passes through the neural network and gives output **f(x)**. Each layer's activation function can be different or the same, except for the last layer, which controls the output type based on the model and problem types (classification or regression). Figure 4.20 shows an example of the backpropagation network.

Step 2: Backpropagation: using a gradient for all layers to update the weights (using the error from the output of step 1 to update all the network weights, from the last layer to the earlier ones). The final layer uses a chain rule with a gradient to calculate new weights, and it continues to the first layer (input layer (w_1)).

4.7.3 Single-Layer Perceptron

It was invented in 1964 by Frank Rosenblatt at Cornell university. It is the simplest feedforward neural network and does not contain any hidden layer. A single-layer perceptron can only learn linear functions. Figure 4.21 shows its architecture.

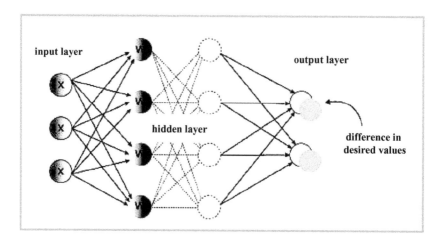

FIGURE 4.20   Backpropagation architecture.

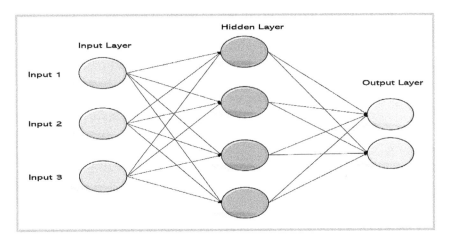

FIGURE 4.21   Single-layer perceptron.

FIGURE 4.22   Multi-layer perceptron.

4.7.4 Multi-Layer Perceptron (MLP)

MLP has more than one hidden layer and is mostly used in classification problems. It is used to learn nonlinear functions. There are three parts to these networks: the input layer, hidden layer, and output layer (Figure 4.22).

4.7.4.1 MLP Example in TensorFlow
Step 1: Import Libraries

```
import tensorflow as tf
import numpy as np
from tensorflow import keras
```

Step 2: Load Data

```
from keras.datasets import mnist
(x _ train, y _ train), (x _ test, y _ test) = mnist.
load _ data()
```

Step 3: One Hot and Normalization Data

```
y_train = tf.one_hot(y_train, 10)
y_test = tf.one_hot(y_test, 10)
x_train = x_train / 255.0
x _ test = x _ test / 255.0
```

Step 4: Making Model

```
model = keras.Sequential([
    keras.layers.Flatten(input_shape=(28, 28)),
    keras.layers.Dense(128, activation='relu'),
    keras.layers.Dropout(.2, input_shape=(2,)),
    keras.layers.Dense(32, activation='relu'),
    keras.layers.Dropout(.2, input_shape=(2,)),
    keras.layers.Dense(10, activation='softmax')])
```

Step 5: Model Summary

```
model.summary()
Model: "sequential"
```

Layer (type)	Output Shape	Param #
flatten_4 (Flatten)	(None, 784)	0
dense_12 (Dense)	(None, 128)	100480
dropout_5 (Dropout)	(None, 128)	0
dense_13 (Dense)	(None, 32)	4128
dropout_6 (Dropout)	(None, 32)	0
dense_14 (Dense)	(None, 10)	330

```
Total params: 104,938
Trainable params: 104,938
Non-trainable params: 0
```

Step 6: Compile the Model

```
model.compile(loss='categorical _ crossentropy',
metrics=['accuracy'], optimizer='adam')
```

Step 7: Train the Model

```
n_val = 5000
n_train = 60000
n_test = 10000
batch_size=100
epochs=100
steps_per_epoch = int((n_train-n_val)/batch_size)
n_val = 5000
validation_split = n_val/n_train
validation_steps = int(n_val / batch_size)
test_steps = int(n_test/batch_size)
history = model.fit(x_train, y_train, epochs=epochs,
steps_per_epoch=steps_per_epoch, validation_split=
validation_split, validation_steps=validation_steps,
callbacks=[tensorboard_callback])
```

Step 8: Test the Model

```
score = model.evaluate(x_test,  y_test, steps=test_
steps, verbose=0)
print('Test loss:', score[0])
print('Test accuracy:', score[1])
```

## CHAPTER 5

Deep Neural Networks (DNNs) Fundamentals and Architectures

5.1 DEEP NEURAL NETWORKS

There are some concepts that you should know when you are working with deep learning algorithms. This chapter reviews the DL models, concepts, and definitions.

5.1.1 What, Is Deep Learning?

Deep learning algorithms (a subset of artificial neural networks (a subset of machine learning)) work with different data types. It processes data through units (neurons) in different ordered sections (layers) by using different techniques in each layer (it imitates the human brain structure and operations). A deep learning structure has several major parameters and hyperparameters to change the learning features, like speed and accuracy. The word "deep" refers to the number of layers (usually, DL architectures have several layers (mostly large) to make it strong and robust to solve complicated real-world problems), which helps the network find more features of the data and help the network to train better.

DOI: 10.1201/9781003025818-5

5.1.2 Deep Learning Needs!

DL algorithms need a large volume of data for training, and the computation costs of making DL model is very high. By solving these two challenges (large data and high computation cost), we can deploy DL algorithms more efficiently.

5.1.3 How to Deploy DL More Efficiently?

There are several important key points to choose and deploy DL architectures correctly and accurately. However, after finding the first trained model, you can optimize it (we discuss it in Chapter 8). These are the most important key points to know how to use DL more efficient:

(a) have a right and proper dataset,

(b) doing the correct and necessary data preprocessing,

(c) choose the correct features of the data,

(d) choosing the best DL algorithm for the problem,

(e) setting up the network's parameters correctly,

(f) setting up the network's hyperparameters correctly, and

(g) defining the correct layers (types and orders).

Here, we present some definitions and concepts that you should know to start working with any deep learning algorithms.

5.1.4 Vanishing Gradient

One of the challenges in using deep learning is the vanishing gradient problem. The gradient is an optimization technique, and when the network's weights are going to be negative, through time, the values of the weights will be very small and close to zero (for the values of the weights that are close to zero, their gradient is zero). This is the problem: the network and its weights cannot be updated, and it will be stuck at a point. So, its name is vanishing gradient because the gradient does not work more in this situation! There are several solutions for this problem, like using **Rectified Linear Unit (ReLU)** that removes the negative values.

5.1.5 Channel

The input data in deep learning can have different channels. For example, if the data are images and use RGB (standard for color image), there are three channels for these data (**Red**, **Green**, and **Blue**).

5.1.6 Embedding

An embedding represents the input data (like image, text, and audio) to a vector. For example, we embed the data like images into the common space, and in sentiment analysis, the embedding process converts words to vectors.

5.1.7 Fine-Tuning

It is a method of initializing a network's parameters for a task and then update these parameters with a new task. For example, there is a pre-trained word embedding in the NLP system (like the word to vector), that its parameters can be updated for a specific task like content analysis or sentiment analysis.

5.1.8 Data Augmentation

Using some methods (depends on the data type) to generate some new data from original data is one of the challenges in DL. For example, flipping and rotation are two methods to create new data.

5.1.9 Generalization

The NN performance mostly depends on generalization potential that it helps generalize the model and gives it this ability to operate with new data. As ANNs, a DL network is better to cover generalization to increase the model flexibility. There are several methods like regularization to increase the generalization.

5.1.10 Regularization

It is a method that, by doing some minor changes in the learning process, generalizes the model better and makes it more flexible. Some of the regularization methods are L_1, L_2, and dropout that we discuss in the next sections.

5.1.11 L_1 and L_2

These are the most popular kinds of regularization methods. Here, in general, we add a term to regularize (regularization term) and update the cost function.

```
Cost function = Loss + Regularization term
```

By increasing these values, the weight value will be decreased to make the model simpler and generalize the model better. There are two main terms as L_1 and L_2. L_2 is:

```
Cost function = Loss + Lambda/2m × ∑ ||w||²
```

The lambda is the hyperparameter. L_2 is known as a weight decay method. It reduces the weights close to zero but not zero. Also, the L_1 is:

```
Cost function = Loss + lambda/2m × ∑ ||w||
```

Usually, we prefer L_2 to L_1, except when we plan to compress the model more (because in L_1, the weights may be reduced to zero).

5.1.12 Dropout

Dropout works by masking (dropping) some nodes in the network in the training step (we will explain in more detail this concept later in this chapter).

5.1.13 End-to-End Learning

Deep learning supports end-to-end learning that helps solves problems more efficiently. For example, recognizing the face using the traditional AI methods or artificial neural networks has some steps such as cropping, translation, detection, and recognition. However, when you are using deep learning, it does not need these steps, and the layers in the network extract the features from data automatically (Chapter 7 provides an implementation example for face recognition by DL).

5.2 DEEP LEARNING APPLICATIONS

Deep learning has the capability to model complicated real-world problems. Its algorithms are not used just for image and audio or some signal data classification. Deep learning algorithms are used in many applications like:

- self-driving cars,
- natural language processing,
- content analysis,
- visual recognition,
- fashion,

- chatbots,

- virtual agents,

- text generation,

- handwritten generation and machine translation,

- advertising, and

- fraud detection.

There are many research and projects for deploying deep learning, from medical image analysis to drug discovery and genomes analysis. Also, based on the data nature and type of the problems, some real-world problems can be solved by deep learning; for example, performing real-time human behavior analysis, translating languages, and forecasting natural catastrophes. The autonomous vehicle is one of the hot topics that many large companies like google, apple, tesla, and uber invest in. The financial industry is another area that used deep learning for fraud detection of money transactions. It saved billions for financial and insurance institutes. By using some information like customer transactions and credit scores, systems classify and detect fraud (Figure 5.1).

These days we use several virtual assistance services like Alexa, Siri, and google assistance in our daily life. These products give you smart services like desired songs or restaurants and interact with you smartly and intelligently. They understand human language and provide you smart

FIGURE 5.1 There are several applications for deep learning techniques.

FIGURE 5.2   Healthcare is one of the new applications of deep learning.

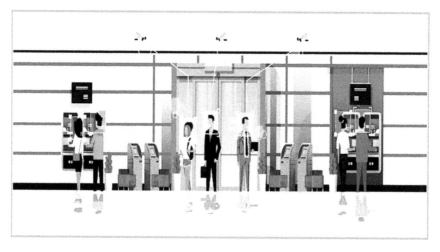

FIGURE 5.3   Virtual assistant robots use deep learning methods.

and autonomous responses. They also give you some services, like reading or writing your email and organizing your documents (Figure 5.2).

We review the implementation steps of a virtual assistant robot in Chapter 7 (Figure 5.3).

5.3 DEEP LEARNING ALGORITHMS AND ARCHITECTURES

When we have a simple neural network with more than one hidden layer, we have deep neural networks (DNNs).

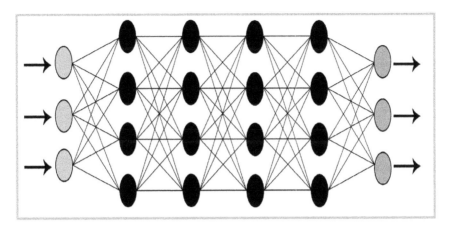

FIGURE 5.4   DNN with four hidden layers.

Figure 5.4 shows an example of DNN. It has one input layer, one output layer, and four hidden layers. Here, we present an example for DNN with TensorFlow for the MNIST dataset. The input image size is 28×28, the hidden activation function is ReLU, and the output activation function is SoftMax.

```
#MNIST Example
#input data and setting the network parameters and
hyper parameters
input_data_shape = (28, 28)
hidden_activation_function = 'relu'
output_activation_function = 'softmax'
# define the model
dnn_Model = models.Sequential()
# input layer
dnn_model.add(ks.layers.Flatten(input_shape = input_
data_shape, name = 'Input_layer'))
# first hidden layer
dnn_model.add(ks.layers.Dense(256, activation =
hidden_activation_function, name = 'Hidden_layer_1'))
# second hidden layer
dnn_model.add(ks.layers.Dense(192, activation =
hidden_activation_function, name = 'Hidden_layer_2'))
# third hidden layer
dnn_model.add(ks.layers.Dense(128, activation =
hidden_activation_function, name = 'Hidden_layer_3'))
```

```
# forth hidden layer
dnn_model.add(ks.layers.Dense(64, activation = hidden_
activation_function, name = 'Hidden_layer_4'))
# output hidden layer
dnn_model.add(ks.layers.Dense(10, activation = output_
activation_function, name = 'Output_layer'))
# model summary
dnn_model.summary()
```

5.3.1 Convolutional Neural Networks (CNNs)

CNN is one of the most popular deep learning algorithms with four main parts:

- convolution filters,
- pooling or subsampling,
- activation (transition) function, and
- fullyconnected layer.

It shows promising results in visual classification problems. Its base is convolution functions (filters), in which each neuron will connect to the output of these filters as the receptive field. We will discuss more in detail about this type of deep learning algorithm in this chapter (Figure 5.5).

5.3.2 Recurrent Neural Networks (RNNs)

RNN is a neural network that usually is used for time series prediction problems. It uses stochastic gradient descent for training. RNNs process

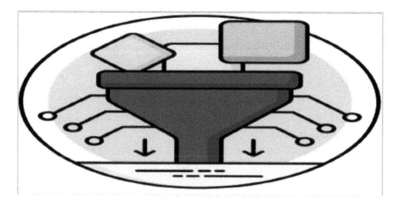

FIGURE 5.5   CNN looks for the features of the data for training.

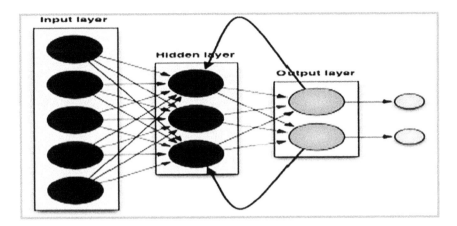

FIGURE 5.6   RNN uses the features of previous layers.

the data using feedforward and return the output values to the hidden and input layer through the backpropagation (storing past data and using them for forecasting).

RNN has several applications, such as predicting an event based on the previous events and data (like the stock market data), and has two main types:

- bidirectional RNN, and

- deep RNN.

RNN shares the same parameters for all layers. It does not work very well in long-term processing and cannot have intense layers. Figure 5.6 shows an RNN architecture and shows how the output layer has a connection with the hidden layer.

5.3.3 Long Short-Term Memory (LSTM)

As we mentioned in the previous section, RNN does not work correctly in long-term processing. LSTM is a type of RNNs that uses backpropagation and has a memory block instead of the neuron for connecting to the layers. It is suitable for many applications such as language translation, sentiment analysis, stock market predictions, and images captioning (Figure 5.7).

5.3.4 Generative Adversarial Networks (GANs)

GAN is an unsupervised learning algorithm that generates new data by self-learning. Its algorithm has two modules: the first one is the generator, which generates a new sample, and the second one is a discriminator to

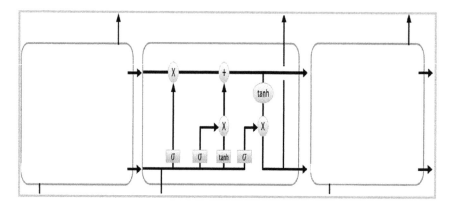

FIGURE 5.7   LSTM is a type of RNNs that uses backpropagation and has memory.

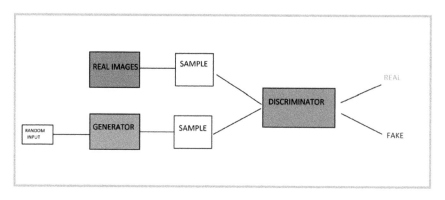

FIGURE 5.8   GAN networks architecture.

classify original from new data (fake data) (these two modules compete with each other).

These models use different loss functions (its computation is very high), and if one of them fails, the whole network fails. The generator and discriminator weights can be updated through iterations. Figure 5.8 shows a general structure of the GAN networks.

5.3.5 Residual Neural Network Learning (ResNets)

ResNet is used for some complicated problems that other methods like CNNs do not work probably. It has several residual modules (layers) that these layers have several functions to operate on input data. In comparison to RNNs, it is more accurate and lighter. Figures 5.9 and Figure 5.10 show the regular networks and ResNet networks architecture. You can see how these two networks are different.

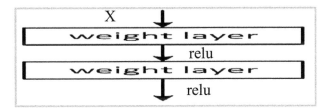

FIGURE 5.9   Regular networks architecture.

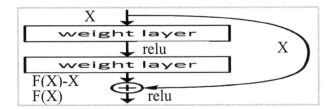

FIGURE 5.10   ResNet networks architecture.

5.4 CONVOLUTIONAL NEURAL NETWORKS (CNNS)

5.4.1 CNN Layers

5.4.1.1 Convolution Layers

The main part of a CNN is convolution layers. When a convolution function processes and moves over the whole data matrix (for example, an image), the output is convolved (filtered). A stride is a value (specific slide) that each time the convolution function moves. For example, stride 2 means the convolution window moves two elements (here it is a pixel) along right or bottom (default is moving from left to right and top to bottom). CNN does filter by using kernels (same size as convolution windows) and multiplying the image pixel values in windows by kernel values. To create a CNN, you should know and determine the number of filters, kernel size, and strides.

If the kernel filter size is 4×4=16, then each neuron (has one bias plus 16 weights) connects to the receptive field. It can have several convolutions layers, which outputs are feature maps. Figure 5.11 shows how a 3×3 filter works. It moves over the original input image, and its values multiply by the masked part of the image's values. For example, here, the convolution output for the first output is -2. Also, Figure 5.12 shows the final output of an original image. You can see the outputs of the filters in each layer.

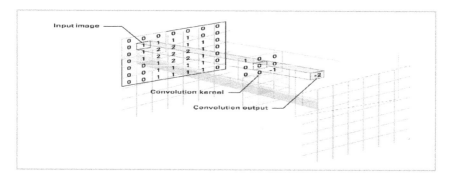

FIGURE 5.11   Convolving by 3×3 filter.

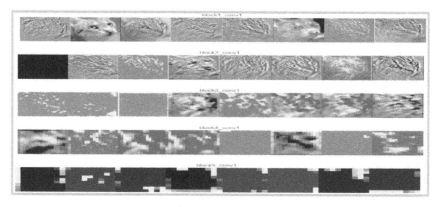

FIGURE 5.12   The outputs of filters.

5.4.1.2 Pooling Layers

CNNs also have pooling (ex. max-pooling, min pooling, and average pooling) layers to find subregions and decrease computational time (Figure 5.13).

The pooling layer functionality depends on the size of the pooling windows and the type of pooling. It operates on the convolution outputs to reduce the size for less operation in the next step.

5.4.1.3 Dropout

It helps networks to memorize and generalize networks for using in different applications. Sometimes removing some neurons, by maintaining the generalization besides keeping the patterns, helps the network performance. These nodes can be removed by making them off. For this purpose, one of the popular ways is to make a random matrix of zero and multiply it by the nodes' values to make them off or on (Figure 5.14).

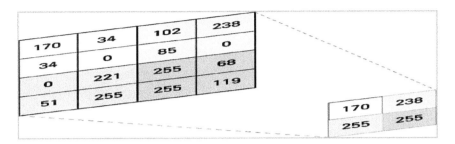

FIGURE 5.13   Max pooling.

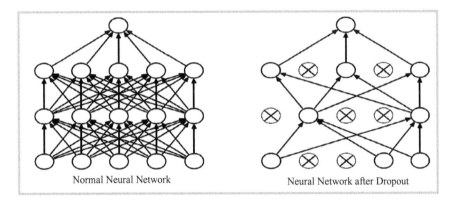

FIGURE 5.14   Dropout example.

Random dropout does not change the weights, and it does mask over the network to drop some nodes. Also, it is used during the training step.

5.4.1.4 Batch Normalization

Normalization techniques are using to make machine learning algorithms more generalized to new sample data. For example, if data have a normal distribution, then centroid the data by subtracting from the mean, and then dividing the result by standard deviation is normalization. Batch normalization is a method that helps to have a deeper network. In batch normalization, the features are normalized by feeding to the batch normalization layer. In general, it has a significant effect on improving training and convergence of speed. However, it is based on the batch's dimension, which leads to a strong dependence on the batch size setting. The deep network data is in a four-dimensional (4D) vector (N, C, H, W) order, where **N** is the batch axis, **C** is the channel axis, **H** and **W** are the spatial height and width axes (Figure 5.15).

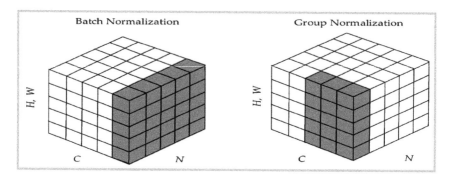

FIGURE 5.15   Batch normalization vs. group normalization.

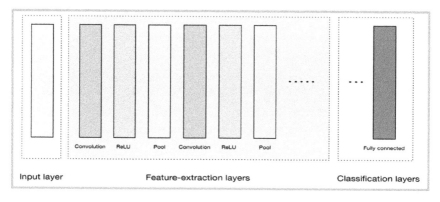

FIGURE 5.16   Fully connected layer.

5.4.1.5 Fully Connected Layer

Fully connected layers are those layers that all nodes in the current layer are connected to the next layer. In DL models, the last few layers are fully connected to construct the output, usually a set of probability values (for example, SoftMax activation). Figure 5.16 shows the layers in CNN (the last fully connected layer is also the classification layer).

5.4.2 Design a CNN

Here we implement a LeNet5 architecture. Let us explain LeNet5. It has a sequence of convolution and pooling layers. It has two fully connected layers and one classifier layer. All other CNNs architecture has almost these implementation steps. Let us go to the coding steps:

Step 1: In the first step, you should determine the libraries you need for implementation and import them. These libraries help you make your code more robust and accurate and make the computation cost less.

```
import TensorFlow as tf
import NumPy as np
from tensorflow.examples.tutorials.mnist import
input _ data
```

Step 2: Setting up the number of samples for the training and testing step and the image size and the number of classes.

```
batch_size = 128
test_size = 256
img_size = 28
num_classes = 10
# define a placeholder for data and y for labels
X = tf.placeholder("float", [None, img_size,
img_size, 1])
Y = tf.placeholder("float", [None, num _ classes])
```

Step 3: Collecting data and creating training and testing category.

```
mnist = mnist_data.read_data_sets("data/")
Xtr, Ytr, Xte, Yte = mnist.train.images, mnist.
train.labels,mnist.test.images, mnist.test.labels
Xtr = Xtr.reshape(-1, img_size, img_size, 1)
Xte = Xte.reshape(-1, img_size, img_size, 1)
#Initialize the weights
def init_weights(shape):
    return tf.Variable(tf.random_normal(shape,
stddev=0.01))
#Weights for layer 1-4
w₁ = init_weights([3, 3, 1, 32])
w₂ = init_weights([3, 3, 32, 64])
w₃ = init_weights([3, 3, 64, 128])
w₄ = init_weights([128 * 4 * 4, 625])
#The output layer is
w _ o = init _ weights([625, num _ classes])
```

Step 4: Define the model.

```
p_keep_conv = tf.placeholder("float")
p_keep_hidden = tf.placeholder("float")
def model(X, w, w₂, w₃, w₄, w_o, p_keep_conv,
p_keep_hidden):
    conv1 = tf.nn.conv2d(X, w,strides=[1, 1, 1, 1],
padding='SAME')
    conv1 = tf.nn.relu(conv1)
    conv1 = tf.nn.max_pool(conv1, ksize=[1, 2, 2, 1]
,strides=[1, 2, 2, 1], padding='SAME')
    conv1 = tf.nn.dropout(conv1, p_keep_conv)
    conv2 = tf.nn.conv2d(conv1, w₂,strides=[1, 1, 1,
1],padding='SAME')
    conv2 = tf.nn.relu(conv2)
    conv2 = tf.nn.max_pool(conv2, ksize=[1, 2, 2,
1],strides=[1, 2, 2, 1],padding='SAME')
    conv2 = tf.nn.dropout(conv2, p_keep_conv)
    conv3 = tf.nn.conv2d(conv2, w₃,strides=[1, 1, 1,
1],padding='SAME')
    conv3_a = tf.nn.relu(conv3)
    FC_layer = tf.nn.max_pool(conv3, ksize=[1, 2, 2,
1],strides=[1, 2, 2, 1], padding='SAME')
    FC_layer = tf.reshape(FC_layer, [-1,w₄.get_
shape().as_list()[0]])
    FC_layer = tf.nn.dropout(FC_layer, p_keep_conv)
    output_layer = tf.nn.relu(tf.matmul(FC_layer, w₄))
    output_layer = tf.nn.dropout(output_layer,
p_keep_hidden)
    result = tf.matmul(output_layer, w_o)
  return result
```

Step 5: Train and evaluate the model.

```
py_x = model(X, w, w₂, w₃, w₄, w_o, p_keep_conv,
p_keep_hidden)
Y_ = tf.nn.softmax_cross_entropy_with_logits(py_x, Y)
cost = tf.reduce_mean(Y_)
optimizer = tf.train.RMSPropOptimizer(0.001, 0.9).
minimize(cost)
predict_op = tf.argmax(py_x, 1)
with tf.Session() as sess:
    tf.initialize_all_variables().run()
    for i in range(100):
```

```
        training_batch =  zip(range(0, len(Xtr),
batch_size), range(batch_size, len(Xtr)+1,
batch_size))
        for start, end in training_batch:
            sess.run(optimizer, feed_dict={X: Xtr
[start:end],Y: Ytr [start:end],p_keep_conv: 0.8,
p_keep_hidden: 0.5})
        test_indices = np.arange(len(Xte))
        np.random.shuffle(test_indices)
        test_indices = test_indices[0:test_size]
        print(i, np.mean(np.argmax(Yte[test _ indices],
axis=1) ==sess.run(predict _ op, feed _ dict={X:
Xte[test _ indices], Y: Yte [test _ indices], p _ keep _
conv: 1.0, p _ keep _ hidden: 1.0})))
```

5.5 RECURRENT NEURAL NETWORKS (RNNS)

For problems with a sequence of data with an order, using a regular neural network is not a good solution, and RNNs can be a good answer. One of the RNNs applications is sentiment analysis to determine whether a sentence or phrase is positive or negative.

5.5.1 Recurrent Neural Network Architecture

Development in deep learning structure and improving computation power make RNN architecture one of the most interesting deep neural networks. RNNs process each element of the sequence, keep its features in its memory, and then process the next element in a sequence. The neuron cell or node in RNNs is connected to another node and to itself.

5.5.2 Long Short-Term Memory (LSTM)

One of the challenges for RNNs happens when iterates over one node in a recursive process, and the weights go small, and then the vanishing gradient happens. In addition, short-term memory is another challenging problem, and these two problems make RNNs improper for long sequence or series processing.

LSTM helps RNNs separate two terms:

- short (input data is mixed of data in sequence) and

- long (choosing data from short memory and addition and multiplication on data).

By doing this, you can remove the vanishing gradient. LSTM is different from RNNs in these three main aspects of controlling:

- inputs data,
- remembering sample data, and
- outputs.

5.5.3 Designing an RNN (LSTM)

Here, we implement an RNN model (LSTM) using TensorFlow and Keras for MNIST database classification. There are five main steps for this implementation as follows.

5.5.3.1 Import Libraries

The first step is to import some libraries like NumPy, TensorFlow, and Keras.

```
import numpy as np
import tensorflow as tf
from tensorflow import keras
from tensorflow.keras import layers
```

5.5.3.2 Load and Normalize the Dataset

Using MNIST as a database, load it, put the data for training and testing categories, and then normalizing it (here, the maximum value is 255).

```
#loading the data
mnist = keras.datasets.mnist
#find the training and testing data
(x_train, y_train), (x_test, y_test) = mnist.
load_data()
#normalizing the data
x_train, x_test = x_train / 255.0, x_test / 255.0
sample, sample _ label = x _ train[3], y _ train[3]
```

5.5.3.3 Build the Model

Each MNIST data (here image data) has 28×28 size, and any batch in the dataset is a tensor with (batch_size, 28, 28) shape. The labels here have values between 0 and 9 (10 labels).

```
batch_size = 64
input_dim = 28
units = 64
```

```
output_size = 10
def build_model(allow_cudnn_kernel=True):
    if allow_cudnn_kernel:
        lstm_layer = keras.layers.LSTM(units, input_
shape=(None, input_dim))
    else:
        lstm_layer = keras.layers.RNN(keras.layers.
LSTMCell(units), input_shape=(None, input_dim) )
    model = keras.models.Sequential([ lstm_layer,
keras.layers.BatchNormalization(), keras.layers.
Dense(output_size),])
    return model
```

5.5.3.4 Train the Model

Compile the model with desired parameters like loss function, optimizer, and metric and then train the model using the test data values.

```
model = build_model(allow_cudnn_kernel=True)
model.compile(loss=keras.losses.SparseCategoricalCross
entropy(from_logits=True),optimizer="adam",metrics=["a
ccuracy"],)
model.fit(x _ train, y _ train, validation _ data=(x _ test,
y _ test), batch _ size=batch _ size, epochs=100)
```

Outputs:

```
Epoch 1/10
938/938 [==============================] - 12s 13ms/
step - loss: 0.3543 - accuracy: 0.8882 - val_loss:
0.1381 - val_accuracy: 0.9555
...
```

5.5.3.5 Evaluate the Model

Check and evaluate the model with some sample data (Figure 5.17).

```
import matplotlib.pyplot as plt
with tf.device("CPU:0"):
    cpu_model = build_model(allow_cudnn_kernel=True)
    cpu_model.set_weights(model.get_weights())
    result = tf.argmax(cpu_model.predict_on_batch(tf.
expand_dims(sample, 0)), axis=1)
    print( "Predicted result is: %s, target result is:
%s" % (result.numpy(), sample_labe)
    plt.imshow(sample, cmap=plt.get _ cmap("gray"))
```

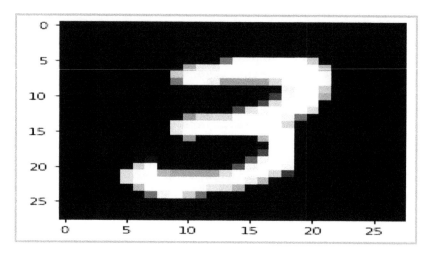

FIGURE 5.17   Model prediction output.

Output:

```
The predicted result is: [3], the target result is: 3
```

5.6 GENERATIVE ADVERSARIAL NETWORK (GANS)

Here, we review the GAN definition, concepts, algorithm and implement an example by GAN to learn how it works.

5.6.1 What is a GAN?

Generative Adversarial Network (GAN) is one of the most recent network architectures in deep learning that; its concept and method give some new advantages in using deep learning algorithms. There are several advantages to use GAN:

- with limited data, it generalizes well,

- it creates some new scenes, and

- it makes more realistic simulated data.

In general, we are doing discrimination (classification) and generation (simulate new scene or data) using discriminative and generative. You can do discrimination in these steps:

1. choose a learning algorithm to learn the classes of data,

2. divide the data into three groups: training, validation, and testing,

3. train the learning algorithm to find the trained model,

4. find the better model using validation data, and

5. test the model using testing data.

The discriminative model learns how to find the boundaries between classes, and the generative model learns each class's distribution. The discriminative model does not work in unsupervised learning and needs more data for better training, and the generative works in unsupervised learning. We can summarize the generative and discriminative goals as follows:

1. **Generative Goal**:

   maximize the similarities that make the discriminator misclassify the fake data as real.

2. **Discriminative Goal**:

   optimizing the differences between real and fake data (training loss close to 0.5).

These are the steps how the generator works:

1. generate some samples (for example, some initial noise data),

2. chose a neural network algorithm (for example, CNN), and

3. train the generator.

A Convolution Neural Network (CNN) can be a discriminator, and you can implement it as follows:

a. chooses a CNN to classify real or fake,

b. has a real dataset and get fake data from a generator,

c. train the CNN on the real and fake data, and,

d. learns to balance the discriminator training with the generator training – if the discriminator is very good, the generator will diverge.

5.6.2 A GAN for Fashion Dataset

Here we present a GAN to learn how it works. These are the general steps:

1. loading dataset,

2. data preprocessing,

3. defining the discriminator model,

4. defining the generator model,

5. combining the generator and discriminator model,

6. training the model, and

7. predict (generate data).

Before starting the first step, as mentioned before, it is better to import some libraries and some platforms to ease your computation, like NumPy, TensorFlow, and Keras.

```
import numpy as np
from matplotlib import pyplot as plt
from tensorflow.keras.models import Model, save_model,
load_model
from tensorflow.keras.layers import Conv2D,
Conv2DTranspose, BatchNormalization, LeakyReLU,
Dropout, Flatten, Dense, Reshape, Input, Embedding,
Concatenate
from tensorflow.keras.utils import plot_model
from tensorflow.keras.optimizers import Adam
from tensorflow.keras.losses import BinaryCrossentropy
```

5.6.2.1 Loading Dataset

The dataset we use here is the fashion MNIST.

```
from keras.datasets.fashion_mnist import load_data
(real_train_images, real_train_labels), (real_test_
images, real_test_labels) = load_data()
print('Train', real_train_images.shape, real_train_
labels.shape)
print('Test', real _ test _ images.shape, real _ test _
labels.shape)
```

the output is:

```
Train (60000, 28, 28) (60000,)
Test (10000, 28, 28) (10000,)
```

5.6.2.2 Data Preprocessing

In this step, you should do some processes on data like normalizing the data, selecting the real data, generating random noise, and selecting the fake data.

a) normalize the data which are between [0, 255] and [-1, 1]

```
def prepare_real_samples(samples):
    prepared_samples = samples.astype('float32')
    prepared_samples = (prepared_samples - 127.5) /
127.5
    return prepared _ samples
```

b) selecting real samples

```
def generate_real_batch(samples, orig_labels,
n_samples):
    indices = np.random.randint(0, samples.shape[0],
n_samples)
    batch_images = samples[indices]
    batch_orig_labels = orig_labels[indices]
    batch_labels = np.full(n_samples,
REAL_LABEL_VALUE)
    return batch _ images, batch _ labels, batch _
orig _ labels.flatten()
```

c) generating random noise as input of the generator

```
def generate_noise_vector(noise_dim, n_samples,
n_classes):
    noise_vector = np.random.normal(size = (n_
samples, noise_dim))
    return noise _ vector, np.random.randint(0, n _
classes, size = n _ samples)
```

d) selecting fake samples

```
def generate_fake_batch(generator, noise_dim, n_
classes, n_samples):
    noise_vector, original_classes = generate_noise_
vector(noise_dim, n_samples, n_classes)
    batch_images = generator.predict([noise_vector,
original_classes])
    batch_labels = np.full(n_samples,
FAKE_LABEL_VALUE)
```

```
     return batch _ images, batch _ labels,
  original _ classes
```

5.6.2.3 Defining the Discriminator Model

You should define the discriminator in this step.

```
def create_discriminator(in_shape = (28, 28, 1),
n_classes = 10, label_smoothing = 0):
    label_input = Input(shape = (1,))
    embedding_input = Embedding(n_classes, LABEL_
EMBEDDING_SIZE)(label_input)
    embedding_input = Dense(in_shape[0] * in_shape[1])
(embedding_input)
    embedding_input = Reshape((in_shape[0], in_
shape[1], 1))(embedding_input)
    image_input = Input(shape = in_shape)
    merge = Concatenate()([image_input,
embedding_input])
    feature_extractor = Conv2D(128, (3,3), strides=(2,
2), padding='same')(merge)
    feature_extractor = LeakyReLU(alpha=0.2)
(feature_extractor)
    feature_extractor = Conv2D(128, (3,3), strides =
(2, 2), padding = 'same')(feature_extractor)
    feature_extractor = LeakyReLU(alpha = 0.2)
(feature_extractor)
    feature_extractor = Flatten()(feature_extractor)
    feature_extractor = Dropout(0.4)
(feature_extractor)
    out_layer = Dense(1, activation = 'sigmoid')
(feature_extractor)
    model = Model([image_input, label_input],
out_layer)
    opt = Adam(learning_rate = 0.0002, beta_1 = .5)
    loss = BinaryCrossentropy(label_smoothing =
label_smoothing)
    model.compile(loss = loss, optimizer = opt,
metrics = ['accuracy'])
    return model
```

you can see the model summary:

```
discriminator = create_discriminator(INPUT_SHAPE,
  N_CLASSES)
discriminator.summary()
```

Layer (type)	Output Shape	Param #	Connected to
input_1 (InputLayer)	[(None, 1	0	
embedding (Embedding)	(None, 1, 50)	500	input_1[0][0]
dense (Dense)	(None, 1, 784)	9984	embedding[0][0]
input_2 (InputLayer)	[(None, 28, 28, 1)]	0	
reshape (Reshape)	(None, 28, 28, 1)	0	ense[0][0]
concatenate (Concatenate)	(None, 28, 28, 2)	0	input_2[0][0]
conv2d (Conv2D)	(None, 14, 14, 128)	2432	concatenate[0][0]
leaky_re_lu (LeakyReLU)	(None, 14, 14, 128)	0	conv2d[0][0]
conv2d_1 (Conv2D)	(None, 7, 7, 128)	147584	leaky_re_lu[0][0]
leaky_re_lu_1 (LeakyReLU)	(None, 7, 7, 128)	0	conv2d_1[0][0]
flatten (Flatten)	(None, 6272)	0	leaky_re_lu_1[0][0]
dropout (Dropout)	(None, 6272)	0	flatten[0][0]
dense_1 (Dense)	(None, 1)	6273	dropout[0][0]

```
Total params: 196,773
Trainable params: 196,773
Non-trainable params: 0
```

5.6.2.4 Defining the Generator Model

You should define the generator in this step:

```
def create_generator(noise_dim = 100, dense_layer_
nodes = LATENT_DENSE_SIZE, n_classes = 10):
    label_input = Input(shape = (1,))
    embedding_input = Embedding(n_classes, LABEL_
EMBEDDING_SIZE)(label_input)
    embedding_input = Dense(LATENT_LOW_RES_VALUE *
LATENT_LOW_RES_VALUE)(embedding_input)
    embedding_input = Reshape((LATENT_LOW_RES_VALUE,
LATENT_LOW_RES_VALUE, 1))(embedding_input)
    latent_input = Input(shape=(noise_dim,))
    noise_input = Dense(dense_layer_nodes)
(latent_input)
    noise_input = LeakyReLU(alpha = 0.2)(noise_input)
    noise_input = Reshape(GENERATOR_INITIAL_SHAPE)
(noise_input)
    merge = Concatenate()([noise_input,
embedding_input])
    gen = Conv2DTranspose(128, (4,4), strides = (2,2),
padding = 'same')(merge)
    gen = LeakyReLU(alpha = 0.2)(gen)
    gen = Conv2DTranspose(128, (4,4), strides = (2,2),
padding = 'same')(gen)
    gen = LeakyReLU(alpha = 0.2)(gen)
    out_layer = Conv2D(1, (7, 7), activation = 'tanh',
padding = 'same')(gen)
    return Model([latent _ input, label _ input],
out _ layer)
```

you can see the model summary:

```
generator = create_generator(NOISE_DIM, LATENT_DENSE_
SIZE, N_CLASSES)
generator.summary()
plot_model(generator, to_file = 'generator_plot.png',
show_shapes = True, show_layer_names = True)
The model is:
```

```
Layer (type)              Output Shape          Param #    Connected to
=================================================================================
input_4
(InputLayer)              [(None, 100)]         0

input_3
(InputLayer)              [(None, 1)]           0

dense_3
(Dense)                   (None, 6272)          633472     input_4[0][0]

embedding_1
(Embedding)               (None, 1, 50)         500        input_3[0][0]

leaky_re_lu_2
(LeakyReLU)               None, 6272)           0          dense_3[0][0]

dense_2
(Dense)                   (None, 1, 49)         2499       embedding_1[0][0]

reshape_2
(Reshape)                 (None, 7, 7, 128)     0          leaky_re_lu_2[0][0]

reshape_1
(Reshape)                 (None, 7, 7, 1)       0          dense_2[0][0]

concatenate_1
(Concatenate)             (None, 7, 7, 129)     0          reshape_2[0][0]

conv2d_transpose
(Conv2DTranspo            (None, 14, 14, 128)   264320     concatenate_1[0][0]

leaky_re_lu_3
(LeakyReLU)               (None, 14, 14, 128)   0          conv2d_transpose[0][0]

conv2d_transpose_1
(Conv2DTrans)             (None, 28, 28, 128)   262272     leaky_re_lu_3[0][0]

leaky_re_lu_4
(LeakyReLU)               (None, 28, 28, 128)   0          conv2d_transpose_1[0][0]

conv2d_2 (Conv2D)         (None, 28, 28, 1)     6273       leaky_re_lu_4[0][0]
=================================================================================
Total params: 1,169,336
Trainable params: 1,169,336
Non-trainable params: 0
```

5.6.2.5 Combining the Generator and Discriminator Model

You should define the combining function for generator and discriminator in this step:

```
def create_gan(generator_model, discriminator_model,
label_smoothing = 0):
    discriminator_model.trainable = False
```

```
    generator_noise, generator_embedding = generator_
model.input
    generator_output = generator_model.output
    gan_output = discriminator_model([generator_
output, generator_embedding])
    model = Model([generator_noise, generator_
embedding], gan_output)
    opti = Adam(lr = 0.0001, beta=0.7)
    loss = BinaryCrossentropy(label_smoothing =
label_smoothing)
    model.compile(loss = loss, optimizer = opt,
metrics = ['accuracy'])
    return model
```

you can see the model summary:

```
gan = create_gan(generator, discriminator)
gan.summary()
plot _ model(gan, to _ file='gan _ plot.png', show _
shapes=True, show _ layer _ names=True)
```

The model is:

Layer (type)	Output Shape	Param #	Connected to
input_4 (InputLayer)	[(None, 100)]	0	
input_3 (InputLayer)	[(None, 1)]	0	
dense_3 (Dense)	(None, 6272)	633472	input_4[0][0]
embedding_1 (Embedding)	(None, 1, 50)	500	input_3[0][0]
leaky_re_lu_2 (LeakyReLU)	(None, 6272)	0	dense_3[0][0]
dense_2 (Dense)	(None, 1, 49)	2499	embedding_1[0][0]
reshape_2 (Reshape)	(None, 7, 7, 128)	0	leaky_re_lu_2[0][0]
reshape_1 (Reshape)	(None, 7, 7, 1)	0	dense_2[0][0]
concatenate_1 (Concatenate)	(None, 7, 7, 129)	0	reshape_2[0][0
conv2d_transpose (Conv2DTransp)	(None, 14, 14, 128)	264320	concatenate_1[0][0]

leaky_re_lu_3 (LeakyReLU)	(None, 14, 14, 128)	0	conv2d_transpose[0][0]
conv2d_transpose_1 (Conv2DTrans)	(None, 28, 28, 128)	262272	leaky_re_lu_3[0][0]
leaky_re_lu_4 (LeakyReLU)	(None, 28, 28, 128)	0	conv2d_transpose_1[0][0]
conv2d_2 (Conv2D)	(None, 28, 28, 1)	6273	leaky_re_lu_4[0][0]
functional_1 (Functional)	(None, 1)	196773	conv2d_2[0][0]

```
=================================================================
Total params: 1,366,109
Trainable params: 1,169,336
Non-trainable params: 196,773
```

5.6.2.6 Create Train Function and Train the Model

```
def train_gan(gan, generator, discriminator, latent_
dim, epochs, batches_per_epoch, batch_size, initial_
image_noise, verbose=1):
    image_noise_decrement = initial_image_noise /
epochs
    image_noise_magnitude = initial_image_noise
    if verbose > 0:
        print(f"Beginning training... {epochs}
epochs, each with {batches_per_epoch} batches of
{batch_size}")
        print(f"Latent vector size {latent_dim}")
        print(f"Image noise initial magnitude: {image_
noise_magnitude}, decay: {image_noise_decrement}")
        print("Training... ")
        print("Metrics: Discriminator Real,
Discriminator Fake, Generator")
    for i in range(epochs):
        train_gan_single_epoch(gan, generator,
discriminator, latent_dim, batches_per_epoch, batch_
size, image_noise_magnitude, verbose=verbose)
        print('the epoch is: ', i)
        image_noise_magnitude -= image_noise_decrement
        if verbose >= 1:
            fake_images, fake_labels, fake_classes =
generate_fake_batch(generator, latent_dim, N_CLASSES,
10)
            disc_fake_classifications = discriminator.
predict([fake_images, fake_classes])
```

```
            fake_images = (fake_images + 1) / 2
            print(f'After {(i+1)*BATCHES*BATCH_SIZE}
samples.')
            print('Image labels are D(image) and
Class(image)')
            print('  Generated Images and
Discriminator Output:')
            for i in range(10):
                ax = plt.subplot(2, 5, i+1)
                ax.axis('off')
                ax.set_title(f'{disc_fake_
classifications[i][0]:.2f}, {fake_classes[i]}')
                plt.imshow(fake_images[i].
reshape(INPUT_SHAPE[0], INPUT_SHAPE[1]))
            plt.tight_layout()
            plt.show()
            print('  Real Images and Discriminator
Output:')
            real_images, real_batch_labels, real_
classes = generate_real_batch(prepared_real_images,
real_train_labels, 10)
            disc_real_classifications = discriminator.
predict([real_images, real_classes])
            real_images = (real_images + 1) / 2
            for i in range(10):
                ax = plt.subplot(2, 5, i+1)
                ax.axis('off')
                ax.set_title(f"{disc_real_
classifications[i][0]:.2f} {real_classes[i]}")
                plt.imshow(real_images[i])
            plt.tight_layout()
            plt.show()
```

Now you can train the model:

```
EPOCHS = 50
BATCHES = 50
BATCH_SIZE = 128
IMAGE_NOISE_START = .1
LABEL_SMOOTHING_MAGNITUDE = .1
#more training for 50 epochs
discriminator = create_discriminator(INPUT_SHAPE, N_
CLASSES, label_smoothing = LABEL_SMOOTHING_MAGNITUDE)
```

```
generator = create_generator(NOISE_DIM, LATENT_DENSE_
SIZE, N_CLASSES)
gan = create_gan(generator, discriminator, label_
smoothing = LABEL_SMOOTHING_MAGNITUDE)
train_gan(
    gan,
    generator,
    discriminator,
    NOISE_DIM,
    EPOCHS,
    BATCHES,
    BATCH_SIZE,
    IMAGE_NOISE_START,
    verbose=2
)
save _ model(generator, 'cgan _ model100.h5')
```

5.6.2.7 Predict (Generate Data)

```
model = load_model('cgan_model100.h5')
fig = plt.figure()
fig.set_size_inches(16, 16)
#display images
def plot(examples, n):
    for i in range(n * n):
        plt.subplot(n, n, 1 + i)
        plt.axis('off')
        plt.imshow(examples[i, :, :, 0],
cmap='gray_r')
    plt.show()
#generate random noise and labels
latent_points, labels = generate_noise_vector(100,
100, 10)
#generating labels according to the category
labels = np.asarray([x for _ in range(10) for x in
range(10)])
#predicting
X = model.predict([latent_points, labels])
#rescaling the predicted image from [-1, 1] to [0, 1]
X = (X + 1) / 2.0
# plot the result
plot(X, 10)
```

CHAPTER 6

Deep Neural Networks (DNNs) for Images Analysis

6.1 DEEP LEARNING AND IMAGE ANALYSIS

Deep learning (DL) algorithms have shown promising results in many applications using different data types, from images to stock market data. The published results of using DL in image analysis show very good performance compared to traditional machine learning methods. DL's algorithms use some visual data features that help to do better training and achieve better models. There are several applications for using DL in image analysis, like autonomous vehicles, medical imaging, privacy, security, and entertainment. In this chapter, we review how to deploy DL's methods for image analysis. We discuss and implement image analysis, object recognition, image classification, image segmentation, and generation projects using DL's algorithms. In each of these examples, we review the problem, then define the model, and, in the end, implement it on a particular dataset (Figure 6.1).

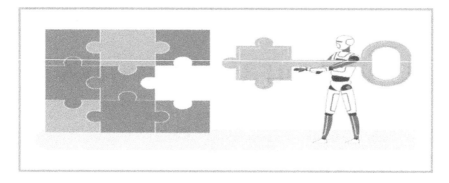

FIGURE 6.1   One of the most interesting DL applications is image analysis.

6.2 CONVOLUTIONAL NEURAL NETWORKS (CNNS) AND IMAGE ANALYSIS

This section explains some critical concepts, such as convolution, pooling, and finding patterns in the images. Usually, the image data have high dimensions; for example, a small image with 28×28 size has 784 pixels. Also, there are different standards for colored images that make their dimension higher. As a standard for colored images, RGB has three basic channels (R=red, G= green, and B=blue). So, if we have a small image (28×28) with three channels, then its dimension is:

$$28 \times 28 \times 3 = 2352$$

Here, the feature vector dimension is 2352 for small image data, and it shows how the computation cost goes very high when we work with large databases. However, some people prefer to use the grayscale image in their works because, in the grayscale images, there is just one channel. For example, in the previous example, it changed the dimension to 784. If we have 10,000 images in our dataset, then:

Three channels: 2,352×10,000= 23,520,000

One channel: 784×10,000 = 7,840,000

Figure 6.2 shows a CNN that extracts different features of the images from different patches in different layers in the **N** dimension space. Several image data patches also show that all their values get a 3D matrix after convolving filters on the image in each layer. If you look at a pixel in an

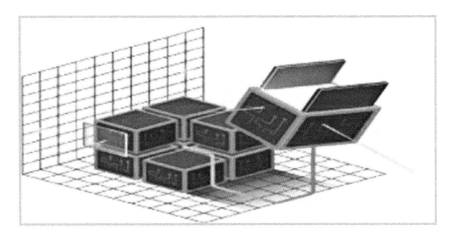

FIGURE 6.2   Image analysis using CNNs.

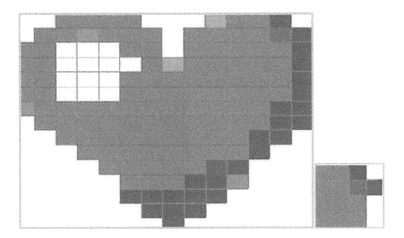

FIGURE 6.3   A pattern in images.

image, you cannot recognize what the image is about, but maybe a set of pixels (a block or patch) give you some information about the picture. Also, each image has several patterns that create its context. Figure 6.3 shows an example that the CNN is looking for the patterns in images (maybe one pixel or even one patch does not show any patterns). The patterns come from any changes in color density and other image data values, and the CNNs filters detect different patterns in the images. They extract these patterns as feature vectors for training the network model. Different filters in different layers provide different feature maps that present different data features. More features make the trained network more accurate for testing its model with real-world problems. When we train a CNN

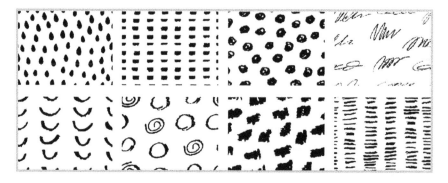

FIGURE 6.4   Different patterns in images.

model, there is a type of hierarchical representation: In the different layers, the different features will be extracted; for example, the early layers extract some patterns like lines and edges, and the last layers extract complex patterns like textures, motif, and the parts of the objects. Sometimes, the trained model can be trained with new data and is used for new tasks. This type of learning is transfer learning that makes the accuracy high and keeps the computation cost reasonable.

If in each layer some patterns exist, their outputs have a higher value, and each layer outputs have less value if the patterns do not exist. The higher values make the probability higher. For example, suppose we are working on a facial recognition system; a layer looks for face segments like nose, lips, eyes, and mouth patterns in their output. If the network finds more patterns, then the probability goes higher for classifying the image as the face. On the other hand, missing these patterns makes the probability of existing a face on an image less. Figure 6.4 shows the different feature maps extracted from the original images (eight feature maps). More layers and more filters make more feature map and make the accuracy better (not always!).

The DL methods for image analysis applications have two main types supervised and unsupervised learning. Also, we categorize the most popular DL applications in image analysis based on these two types of learning methods:

1. supervised learning

- object detection,
- image classification, and
- image segmentation.

2. unsupervised learning

- image generation

There are different algorithms for these applications. Table 6.1 shows some of these methods and algorithms.

6.2.1 Filter Parameters

Some filter parameters like size, type, and stride can be changed and affect the learning process and the network's performance. Here we review these parameters in more detail to learn how they can change the network performance.

6.2.1.1 Number and Type of the Filters

As we mentioned, the outputs of the filters are the feature maps. Each filter is designed to extract and detect a specific pattern. For example, some filters are for extracting the lines, and some of them are for extracting the colors. The filters can be more customized, for example, extracting vertical or horizontal lines. The type of filter (which extracts the features) has a dependency on the problem and the kind of data. We can use as many filters as possible in each layer, but the point is more filters in each layer, making the classification more accurate (not always), but on the other side, it makes the computation cost higher. There is not any rule of thumb that shows the relations between the number of filters and performance. It is coming from the experiments, and it can be different from one problem to another. You can find these numbers for your architecture (based on your problem) by doing more tests. When you start creating your architecture, you can start with basic network architecture and then, by adding and

TABLE 6.1   Most Popular DL Methods for Image Analysis

Task	Model Architectures	Frameworks
object detection	R-FCN, Faster R-CNN	TensorFlow
image classification	VGG, Inception, ResNet	TensorFlow, PyTorch, Keras
image segmentation	Generic segmentation: DeepLab, PSPNet Medical image segmentation: U-Net, HyperDense-Net segmentation: Mask RCNN	TensorFlow, PyTorch
image generation	DCGAN, CycleGAN, ProGAN, BigGAN	-

changing the number and type of the filters, find the best architecture for your problem. Please keep in mind that there are some verified and well-known architectures in CNN that you can use for your problem. For learning purposes, we suggest you target a problem and then create your basic network and try to find its bottlenecks to make its performance better. Now try the results with one of the popular trained CNN algorithms or pre-trained networks and compare your results.

6.2.1.2 Filters Size

The size of the filters can be small or large! The most popular size is 3×3. By choosing a larger size, finding larger patterns is possible (for keeping the output size in each layer, you can pad the image with some zero value around it (Figure 6.5)). For example, if we use 5×5 with the same stride, it makes the computation cost higher because it should multiply with more pixels, and it does not make the process faster when the stride is the same. Also, we should keep the symmetry, and by choosing some even numbers like 2 and 4, it does not cover the symmetry (for dividing the previous layer pixels over the output pixel). On the other hand, in the last layer, some distortion across the layer can happen. So, among these numbers for filter size (2, 3, 4, and 5), the best value is 3.

6.2.1.3 Stride and Padding Size

Stride is the value that filters move over the image in each processing step. For example, if the stride is one, then the kernel window moves one pixel each time (the stride values are integer and the minimum, and the most

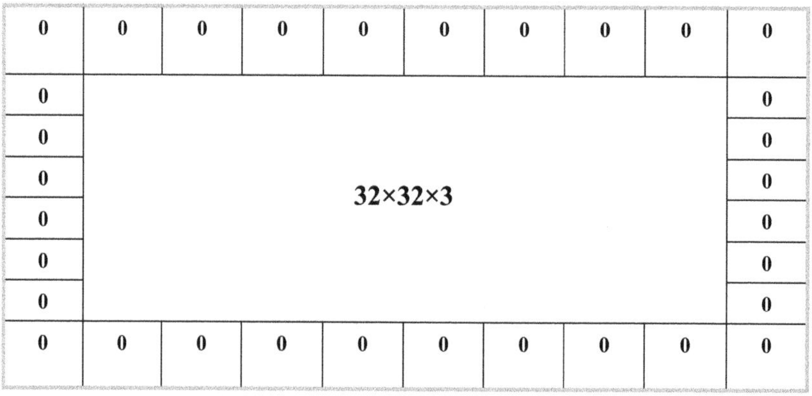

FIGURE 6.5 Padding one around the image with zero values.

popular value is one). The larger value for stride makes the output smaller (we discuss its size more in the next section), and there are possibilities to lose some patterns and information on data.

Another concept is padding, which is adding blank pixels to the image frame. Padding increases the image size and prevents losing information in the image frame when the kernel moves over the image data frame. For example, Figure 6.5 shows a padding one around the 32×32×3 image that their values are zero (zero paddings).

If you choose the stride large, it may make the computation cost less, but it also affects the filter performance in extracting the feature in the convolution process. The most popular size for padding and stride is one. You can try different values to find how those values change the model performance.

6.2.2 Number of Parameters

Here we review the number of parameters in each layer and explain how many parameters exist in each layer. We check the input, convolutional, pooling, and the fully connected layer's parameters.

6.2.2.1 Input Layer

There are no parameters in this layer for learning (in this layer, we have input data). However, there are some discussions about the input data and their size. Also, sometimes before passing the data to the network, after preprocessing, you can add a dimension to the data (training and testing) to make a tensor (matrix) for easier computation in the model training and testing. Figure 6.6 shows the main steps in converting an image to a vector. The feature vectors are the value that the learning models deploy for training.

6.2.2.2 Convolutional Layer

There are different convolutional layers in the CNN architectures. If **I** be the number of input feature maps (previous layer filters) and **O** is the

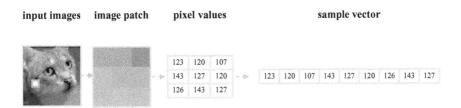

input images	image patch	pixel values			sample vector								
		123	120	107									
		143	127	120	123	120	107	143	127	120	126	143	127
		126	143	127									

FIGURE 6.6   Input images to vector.

number of output feature maps (current layer filters), and **n×m** is the filter size, then the total number of parameters are:

```
total parameters = ((n x m x I) + 1) x O
```

+1 is added because of the bias. For example: if I =32 and O= 64 if the n=3 and m=3, then the total parameters for one convolution layer with these values are:

```
((n x m x I) + 1) x O = ((3 x 3 x 32) + 1) x 64 = 18, 496
```

Figure 6.7 shows four different feature maps from four filters. You can see how these four filters extract different feature maps and what the differences are.

6.2.2.3 Pooling Layer

There are no parameters for learning in this layer, but it has computation cost, which can affect the learning performance. Therefore, choosing the pooling layer size wisely and putting it correctly in the architecture and the right place can improve performance.

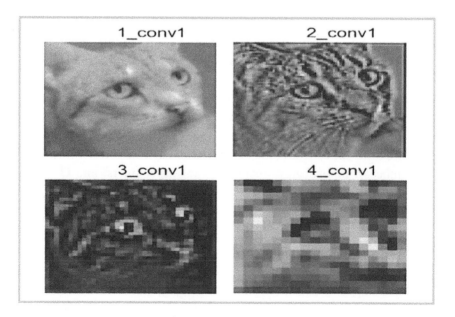

FIGURE 6.7 Four different filters on one image.

6.2.2.4 Fully Connected Layer (FC)

All inputs and outputs have separable weights. Therefore, the number of weights based on the inputs and outputs plus the bias is:

$$((C \times P) + 1 \times C)$$

The current layer neuron number is **C** or output **(O)**, and the previous layer neuron number is **P** or input **(I)**. The output of each layer is:

```
input _ size - (filter _ size - 1)
```

For example, if the input is an image and the image size is 28×28, and the filter size is 3×3, then the output of the layer is:

```
(28 - (3 - 1)) = 26
```

Let us have a general example of a model. If the input is an image with a size of 28×28 and the shape of 28×28×1, it has no parameters.

Assume these values:

```
stride=1,
kernel_ size=3×3,
number of filters in the first layer =32,
then the number of the parameters are:

((kernel_size) × stride + 1) × number of filters)
C₁: 3×3×1+1×32
= 320
```

In the next layer, we already have 32 learned filters from the previous layer, and then the number of trainable parameters is:

$$C_2 : 3 \times 3 \times 32 + 1 \times 32 = 9,248$$
$$C_3 : 3 \times 3 \times 32 + 1 \times 64 = 18,496$$

And so on. The total parameters are the sum of all these values. For example, in these three layers, there are 28,064 parameters:

$$C_1 + C_2 + C_3 = 320 + 9,248 + 18,496 = 28,064$$

Calculating the number of network parameters is a part of validating a good network architecture. After making your model by using the summary, you can check the number of the parameters in each layer in detail in TensorFlow. We plan to review the most popular types of CNN architecture. As mentioned before, you can create your architecture from scratch and then compare your results with these common architectures' outputs and choose the best one.

6.2.3 Imagenet Challenge

Since 2010, a contest: **I**mageNet **L**arge **S**cale **V**isual **R**ecognition **C**hallenge (**ILSVRC**), has been designed for testing different algorithms. The first classification rate was 25%, and the best first achievement was belonging to the AlexNet, which achieved a 10% error rate (however, the recent advanced algorithms show better results). Also, there is a visual database with more than 14 million images for a visual recognition research project in this competition that people use to compare their results.

6.2.4 CNN Architecture

This section presents some of the most popular CNN algorithms. There are several different architectures with different performances. The most significant differences between these architectures are in:

- number of layers,
- elements in each layer, and
- the connection between the layers.

These three parameters define your model and include identifying the network parameters and hyperparameters.

6.2.4.1 LeNet-5 (1998)

This network is one of the simplest deep neural networks that presented in 1998 and has seven layers:

- two convolutional,
- three fully connected layers, and
- two pooling layers.

Its first application was for a handwritten recognition system (2+3+2=7 layers), and it had about 6,000 parameters (6 filters×32×32= 6,144).

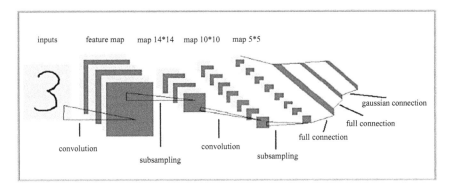

FIGURE 6.8   The LeNet5 network architecture.

Figure 6.8 shows its architecture in more detail. Let's discuss more details about its filters and parameters. If the stride is one, the total parameters are:

$$(n + 2p - f)/s + 1 \times (n + 2p - f)/s + 1 \times Nc$$

where:

Nc: is the number of channels (number of filters used to convolve inputs),

p: padding (no padding in LeNet-5),

s: stride.

Then the number of the parameters is:

$$= \left(32 + 0 - 5\right)/1 + 1 \times \left(32 + 0 - 5\right)/1 + 1 \times 6$$
$$= 28 \times 28 \times 6 = 4{,}704$$

6.2.4.2 AlexNet (2012)

AlexNet is one of the first deep learning methods presented in ImageNet that won it in 2012. You can see its DL architecture in Figure 6.9. Its architecture is like LeNet with more layers (deeper).

They presented dropout techniques for making the computation cost less and achieved better results in comparison to other methods. They also used ReLU in their methods to make the performance better. They used max-pooling layers to make their methods faster. Its architecture has eight layers and include:

- five convolutional layers,

- three fully connected layers with 60 million parameters, and

- ReLU

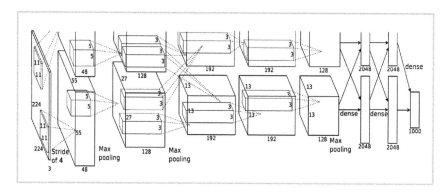

FIGURE 6.9   The AlexNet network architecture.

6.2.4.3 GoogleNet/Inception-v1 (2014)

GoogleNet is a CNN with 22 layers in total. Its pretrained version is available, and you can download and use it. Figure 6.10 shows its architecture.

It won ILSVRC 2014 with an error rate of less than 7%. Its architecture uses some techniques such as batch normalization to reduce the parameters to 4–5 million. In addition, it has some inception (used from the next version) modules, consisting of parallel convolutional filters in each layer. As you can see in Figure 6.10, its network is very deep that it makes the accuracy higher, but its computation cost is also high on the other side.

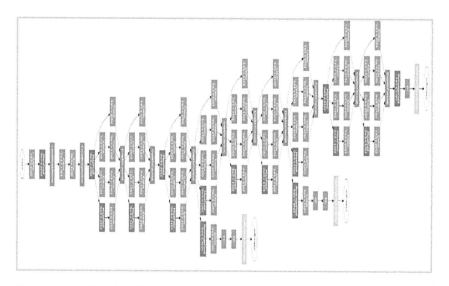

FIGURE 6.10   The GoogleNet network.

6.2.4.4 VGGNet-16 (2014)

VGGNet-16 is a CNN that was presented in 2014 and had 16 layers in its architecture. It achieved 92.7% accuracy on the test image on ImageNet. It is an improvement of AlexNet by replacing large kernel filters. It is very slow to train, and its weights are very large. It has been used for many image classification problems and has shown very interesting results. You can implement it with the current DL platforms like TensorFlow, Keras, or Pytorch. Figure 6.11 shows its architecture. Its architecture includes:

- 13 convolutional layers, and

- three fully connected layers.

It has 138M parameters that take about 500 MB space (maybe the simplest way to improve performance is increasing the layers).

As you can see in Figure 6.11, there are three fully connected layers and 13 convolutional layers.

6.2.4.5 Inception-v3 (2015)

It is the next generation of Inception-v1 (after Inception-v2 with some tweaks in loss function and using some other techniques like batch normalization). It has 24M parameters, and it is a CNN that is used for image analysis and

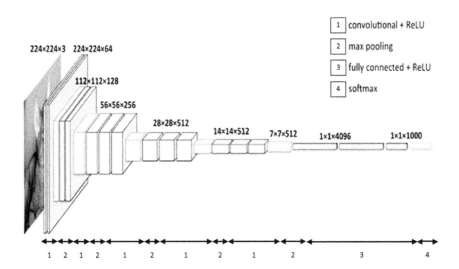

FIGURE 6.11   The VGGNet-16 network.

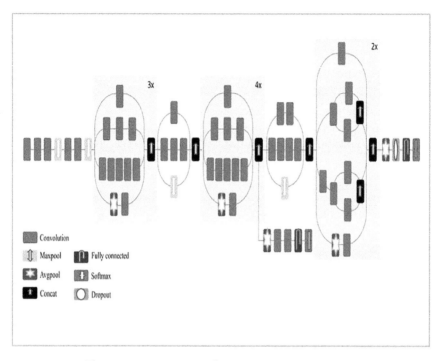

FIGURE 6.12   The Inception-v3 network.

object classification. It has presented by google in 2015 and showed very good results on the ImageNet dataset. Figure 6.12 shows its architecture and is the third version of the first algorithm presented by google.

It has 46 convolution layers and two fully connected layers, and two SoftMax layers. Although, as you can see in Figure 6.12, there are different levels of the convolution layers in some parts of the architecture that their output in total makes the following layer's inputs. In addition, there is a connecting layer that makes these inputs for the next layer.

6.2.4.6 ResNet (2015)

With just increasing the network depth, the accuracy cannot increase more than a threshold. This network, presented by Microsoft, solves ResNet's problem using a shortcut connection (residual) to build a deeper network. ResNet won ILSVC in 2015 with less than a 3.6% error rate with 152 layers. It is a very deep CNN method. Figure 6.13 shows three architecture and compares VGG-19 with 34-layer plain and 34-layer residuals to illustrate this complexity. It has been used in several computer vision applications.

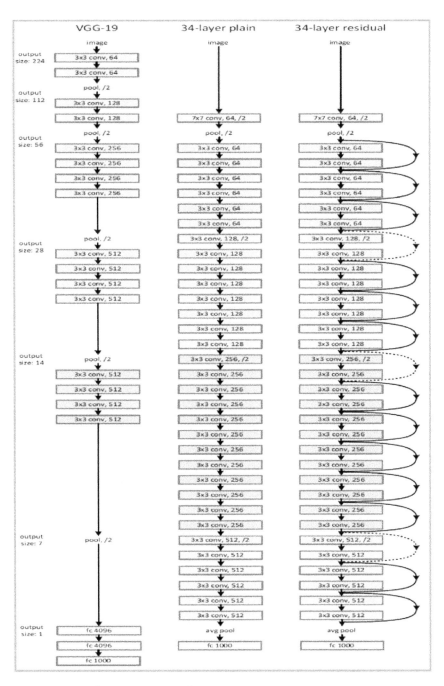

FIGURE 6.13   The ResNet network.

6.2.4.7 Inception-v4 (2016)

The improvement of the Inception-v3 is Inception-v4 that presented by google in 2016 and has these changes in its architecture:

- stem module changes,

- more inception modules, and

- every module uses the same number of filters.

It is a convolutional neural network architecture that reduces the complexity of the inception-v3, but its performance is like the V3. It achieved a 3.08 percent top-5 error on ImageNet in 2016. It has been used in several computer vision applications and showed very good results. You can implement it with several DL platforms like TensorFlow, Keras, and Pytorch. Figure 6.14 shows its architecture.

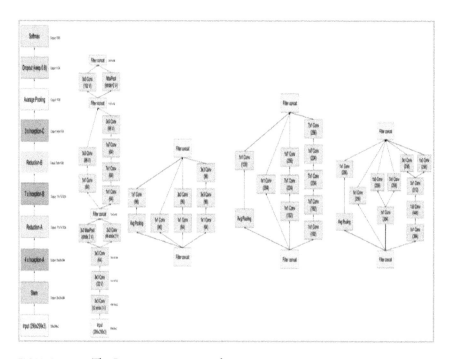

FIGURE 6.14   The Inception-v4 network.

6.3 GENERAL STRATEGY TO IMPLEMENT MODEL USING CNNS

There are some common steps for making a model using DL that, at first, we review these steps. Now, you should think about the architecture that you plan to use in your model. We discussed the most popular CNN architectures in the previous lesson. Then, you can easily deploy all models using Keras, compare the results, and choose the proper architecture in your model. The model implementation using CNN has five steps:

Step 1: import libraries,

Step 2: load the data,

Step 3: define model,

Step 4: train the model, and

Step 5: test the model.

6.3.1 Import Libraries

In any program, the first step is to import libraries to use their methods in our program. These libraries help us to do computing and plotting easier. For example, NumPy, panda, TensorFlow, and Keras are the most popular libraries used in DL modeling (here CNN) using python.

6.3.2 Load the Data and Create the Data Categories

Here, at the first step, we create two folders for data type to process the data. Some preprocessing on the data can make computation costs less. For example, cropping (for removing unnecessary parts of the image) or changing contrast (to make the image quality better). If the problem is supervised learning, we need labeled data (like the dataset with cat and dog data and are already labeled).

We can split the dataset into the training, validation, and testing data (there are some common ratios for data splitting percentage):

- 70% train, 15% validation, and 15% test;

- 80% train, 10% validation, and 10% test; and

- 60% train, 20% validation, and 20% test.

In the model implementation, we may check all these values and see the model's performance.

6.3.3 Make the Model

Choosing or defining the right model is very important. At first, we should decide about the type of architecture. It depends on the type of the problem and the nature of the data in the problem. In the next step, after choosing the right DL architecture, we should define the architecture parameters and hyperparameters. Some of them can be defined at the start of the design, like the number and the type of layers, and some of them, like learning rates, can be defined and fixed through the implementation.

6.3.4 Train the Model

After designing the model, a part of the data (training data) should be used to train the first model. The key point in the training step is the number of data and iteration. The data and their features are very important in the training step. If we extract the correct feature and define the proper architecture, the model can be trained correctly and reasonably. One needs to get better results in DL is the need to a large amount of data in the case of a low volume of data; some methods like data augmentation can be used to generate data (data augmentation has shown its positive effect on the performance, even in case we have a large amount of data).

6.3.5 Test the Model

Testing is one of the main steps in generating any final model. We test each module in the software production steps in the machine learning modeling and implementation steps (like other software production). After training the model and finding the first model, we should test it before using the trained model with the new real-world data. There are still two steps here, validation and testing. In the validation step, we check the model performance with a part of the original data (in the case we did not get our desire performance, modify the model), and in the end, test it with the test data.

6.4 OBJECT RECOGNITION USING CNNS

Object recognition is one of the best examples of using CNN for a real-life problem. Before feeding data to the CNN, we should collect or choose the database and then do some preprocessing on data to prepare them and then use them for our learning algorithm. Also, we deploy several frameworks and libraries to define the CNN model.

6.4.1 Import Libraries

Importing libraries, as the first step, helps us to make the computation easier. In this example, we use TensorFlow and Keras libraries to import.

```
import numpy as np
import pandas as pd
import matplotlib.pyplot as plt
from tensorflow.keras.utils import to_categorical
from tensorflow.keras.models import Sequential
from tensorflow.keras.layers import Dense,Conv2D,MaxPo
ol2D,Flatten
from tensorflow.keras.callbacks import EarlyStopping
from sklearn.metrics import classification_report,
confusion_matrix
from PIL import Image
import seaborn as sns
```

6.4.2 Load the Data and Generate a Dataset

These are some available datasets. At first, load the dataset and split them into three parts (training, validation, and testing). These are the objects in the CIFAR10: airplane, automobile, bird, cat, deer, dog, frog, horse, ship, and truck (Figure 6.15).

FIGURE 6.15   The images on the dataset.

```
(X_train, y_train), (X_test, y_test) = cifar10.
load_data()
y_cat_test = to_categorical(y_test, num_classes=10)
y _ cat _ train = to _ categorical(y _ train,
num _ classes=10)
```

One good coding practice and habit is to write some tests for each part of code to check code. You can also do some data visualization to see the data samples (to see some features like quality and distribution of data) and use some data augmentation methods to generate data variations, which may help train the model better and increase the accuracy.

6.4.3 Make the Model

Now we can define the model architecture. We can add the convolution, pooling, ReLU, and SoftMax layers. In this example, there are two convolution layers, one Max pooling layer, one ReLU, and one SoftMax layer. The input size data are 32×32 in three channels. The pooling windows size is 2×2.

```
model = Sequential()
model.add(Conv2D(filters=32, kernel_size=(4,4),
strides=(1,1), padding='valid', input_shape=(32,32,3),
activation="relu"))
model.add(Conv2D(filters=32, kernel_size=(4,4),
strides=(1,1), padding='valid', input_shape=(32,32,3),
activation="relu"))
model.add(MaxPool2D(pool_size=(2, 2)))
model.add(Flatten())
model.add(Dense(256,activation="relu"))
model.add(Dense(10, activation="softmax"))
model.compile(loss="categorical _ crossentropy",
optimizer="adam", metrics=["accuracy"])
```

We can check the model architecture and the parameters as follows:

```
model.summary()
Model: "sequential"
```

Layer (type)	Output Shape	Param #
conv2d (Conv2D)	(None, 29, 29, 32)	1568

max_pooling2d (MaxPooling2D)	(None, 14, 14, 32)	0
conv2d_1 (Conv2D)	(None, 11, 11, 32)	16416
max_pooling2d_1 (MaxPooling2	(None, 5, 5, 32)	0
flatten (Flatten)	(None, 800)	0
dense (Dense)	(None, 256)	205056
dense_1 (Dense)	(None, 10)	2570

```
=========================================================
Total params: 225,610
Trainable params: 225,610
Non-trainable params: 0
```

6.4.4 Train the Model

Train the model using Keras and TensorFlow by setting up some parameters and hyperparameters like epoch and define the type of optimizer, loss function, and accuracy metric.

```
early_stop = EarlyStopping(monitor="val_loss",
patience=2)
model.fit(X _ train,y _ cat _ train, epochs = 15,
validation _ data = (X _ test, y _ cat _ test), callbacks =
[early _ stop])
```

6.4.5 Test the Model

In the last step, you can test your model using the test data and evaluate your model. Here the model can test using cat data or the test data that are in one folder as test data.

```
metrics = pd.DataFrame(model.history.history)
model.evaluate(X_test, y_cat_test, verbose = 0)
predictions = model.predict_classes(X_test)
plt.figure(figsize=(12,10))
sns.heatmap(confusion _ matrix(y _ test, predictions),
annot=True)
```

Figure 6.16 shows the confusion matrix of the trained model that was tested by test data.

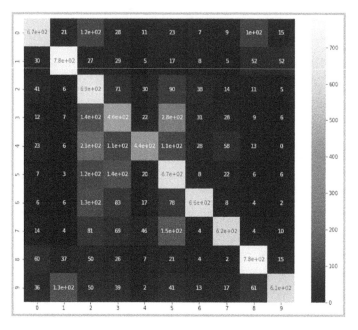

FIGURE 6.16   The confusion matrix.

6.5 IMAGE CLASSIFICATION USING CNNS

Another application of CNN is in image classification. Here, we explain image classification steps using CNN, with example.

6.5.1 Import Libraries

We use TensorFlow, Keras, and matplotlib for implementing the network and visualization in this example.

```
import tensorflow as tf
from tensorflow.keras import datasets, layers, models
import matplotlib.pyplot as plt
```

6.5.2 Load the Data

We do database (cifar10) categorization (train and test data) and data normalization in this step (Figure 6.17).

```
(train_images, train_labels), (test_images, test_
labels) = datasets.cifar10.load_data()
# Normalize pixel values to be between 0 and 1
train_images, test_images = train_images / 255.0,
test_images / 255.0
```

FIGURE 6.17   The CIFAR10 data.

```
class_names = ['airplane', 'automobile', 'bird',
'cat', 'deer','dog', 'frog', 'horse', 'ship', 'truck']
plt.figure(figsize=(10,10))
for i in range(25):
    plt.subplot(5,5,i+1)
    plt.xticks([])
    plt.yticks([])
    plt.grid(False)
    plt.imshow(train_images[i], cmap=plt.cm.binary)
    plt.xlabel(class_names[train_labels[i][0]])
plt.show()
```

6.5.3 Make the Model

Our model has three convolution layers, and we are using max-pooling and ReLU in this example for subsampling and activation function.

```
model = models.Sequential()
model.add(layers.Conv2D(32, kernel_size=(3, 3),
activation='relu', input_shape=(32, 32, 3)))
model.add(layers.MaxPooling2D(pool_size=(2, 2)))
```

```
model.add(layers.Conv2D(64, kernel_size=(3, 3),
activation='relu'))
model.add(layers.MaxPooling2D(pool_size=(2, 2)))
model.add(layers.Conv2D(128, kernel_size=(3, 3),
activation='relu'))
model.add(layers.MaxPooling2D(pool_size=(2, 2)))
model.add(layers.Dropout(0.2))
model.add(layers.Flatten())
model.add(layers.Dense(256, activation='relu'))
model.add(layers.Dense(128, activation='relu'))
model.add(layers.Dense(10, activation='softmax'))
model.summary()
```

Here is the summary of the model that shows the network structure and the total and trainable parameters.

Layer (type)	Output Shape	Param #
conv2d_12 (Conv2D)	(None, 30, 30, 32)	896
max_pooling2d_11 (MaxPooling	(None, 15, 15, 32)	0
conv2d_13 (Conv2D)	(None, 13, 13, 64)	18496
max_pooling2d_12 (MaxPooling	(None, 6, 6, 64)	0
conv2d_14 (Conv2D)	(None, 4, 4, 128)	73856
max_pooling2d_13 (MaxPooling	(None, 2, 2, 128)	0
dropout_3 (Dropout)	(None, 2, 2, 128)	0
flatten_5 (Flatten)	(None, 512)	0
dense_12 (Dense)	(None, 256)	131328
dense_13 (Dense)	(None, 128)	32896
dense_14 (Dense)	(None, 10)	1290

```
Total params: 258,762
Trainable params: 258,762
Non-trainable params: 0
```

6.5.4 Train the Model

In this step, we compile and train the model by determining some parameters like an optimizer, loss function, and accuracy metric.

```
model.compile(optimizer='adam',loss='sparse_
categorical_crossentropy', metrics=['accuracy'])
history = model.fit(train _ images, train _ labels,
epochs=10,  validation _ data=(test _ images,
test _ labels))
```

6.5.5 Test the Model

We do model evaluation using the test data in this step.

```
test _ loss, test _ acc = model.evaluate(test _ images,
test _ labels, verbose=2)
```

6.6 IMAGE SEGMENTATION

Image segmentation is partitioning the segments that are meaningful and help to analyze the images better and easier. Several traditional image segmentation methods do the segmentation based on the image color, intensity, or texture. Image segmentation is one of the image analysis applications of CNN. Here, we implement an example to show you how CNN can help us in image segmentation.

6.6.1 Import Libraries

We use TensorFlow, python, and matplotlib libraries in this section for model generation and visualization.

```
#importing the libraries
from tensorflow_examples.models.pix2pix import pix2pix
import tensorflow_datasets as tfds
from IPython.display import clear_output
import matplotlib.pyplot as plt
```

6.6.2 Load the Data and Generate a Dataset

We should load and split data to the train and test data, resize the data, find the proper mask, and normalize data.

```
# load the data
def load_image_train(datapoint):
  input_image1 = tf.image.resize(datapoint['image'],
(128, 128))
```

```
    input_mask1 = tf.image.
resize(datapoint['segmentation_mask'], (128, 128))
    if tf.random.uniform(()) > 0.5:
      input_image1 = tf.image.
flip_left_right(input_image1)
      input_mask1 = tf.image.
flip_left_right(input_mask1)
    input_image1, input_mask1 = normalize(input_image1,
input_mask1)
    return input_image1, input_mask1
train_lenght1 = info.splits['train'].num_examples
# define the dataset categories
batch_size= 64
buffer_size = 1000
steps_per_epoch = train_lenght1 // batch_size
train = dataset['train'].map(load_image_train, num_
parallel_calls=tf.data.experimental.AUTOTUNE)
test = dataset['test'].map(load_image_test)
train_dataset = train.cache().shuffle(BUFFER_SIZE).
batch(BATCH_SIZE).repeat()
train_dataset = train_dataset.prefetch(buffer_size=tf.
data.experimental.AUTOTUNE)
test _ dataset = test.batch(BATCH _ SIZE)
```

6.6.3 Segmentation Map

Here we define the true mask based on the input image. Figure 6.18 shows the original and true mask of an image.

```
#set the output display
def display(display_list):
  plt.figure(figsize=(15, 15))
  title1 = ['Input Image', 'True Mask', 'Predicted Mask']
  for i in range(len(display_list)):
    plt.subplot(1, len(display_list), i+1)
    plt.title1(title1[i])
    plt.imshow(tf.keras.preprocessing.image.
array_to_img(display_list[i]))
    plt.axis('off')
  plt.show()
for image, mask in train.take(24):
  sample_image, sample_mask = image, mask
display([sample _ image, sample _ mask])
```

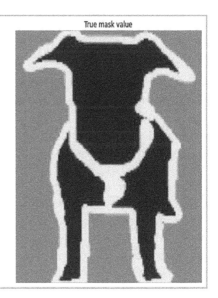

FIGURE 6.18   The mask value of the input image.

6.6.4 Make the Model

Now we define the model that has convolution and pooling layers. The input images have three channels, and their size is 128×128.

```
OUTPUT_CHANNELS = 3
base_model = tf.keras.applications.MobileNetV2(input_
shape=[128, 128, 3], include_top=False)
# Use the activations of these layers
layer_names = [
    'block_1_expand_relu',
    'block_3_expand_relu'
    'block_6_expand_relu',
    'block_13_expand_relu'
    'block_16_project'
]
layers = [base_model.get_layer(name).output for name
in layer_names]
# Create the feature extraction model
down_stack = tf.keras.Model(inputs=base_model.input,
outputs=layers)
down_stack.trainable = False
up_stack = [
    pix2pix.upsample(512, 3),
```

```
        pix2pix.upsample(256, 3),
        pix2pix.upsample(128, 3),
        pix2pix.upsample(64, 3),
]
def unet_model(output_channels):
    inputs = tf.keras.layers.Input(shape=[128,128,3    ])
    x = inputs
# Downsampling
    skips = down_stack(x)
    x = skips[-1]
    skips = reversed(skips[:-1])
# Upsampling
    for up, skip in zip(up_stack, skips):
        x = up(x)
        concat = tf.keras.layers.Concatenate()
        x = concat([x, skip])
# This is the last layer
    last = tf.keras.layers.Conv2DTranspose(
        output_channels, 3, strides= 2,
        padding= 'same' )
    x = last(x)
    return tf.keras.Model(inputs=inputs, outputs=x)
base _ model.summary()
```

The model summary shows the network architecture and the number of trainable and total parameters. The network here is large, but it is interesting to follow.

Layer (type)	Output Shape	Param #	Connected to
input_1 (InputLayer)	[(None, 128, 128, 3)	0	
Conv1_pad (ZeroPadding2D)	(None, 129, 129, 3)	0	input_1[0][0]
Conv1 (Conv2D)	(None, 64, 64, 32)	864	Conv1_pad[0][0]
bn_Conv1 (BatchNormalization)	(None, 64, 64, 32)	128	Conv1[0][0]
Conv1_relu (ReLU)	(None, 64, 64, 32)	0	bn_Conv1[0][0]
expanded_conv_ depthwise (Depthw	(None, 64, 64, 32)	288	Conv1_relu[0][0]

expanded_conv_ depthwise_BN (Bat	(None, 64, 64, 32)	128	expanded_conv_depthwise[0][0]
expanded_conv_ depthwise_relu (R	(None, 64, 64, 32)	0	expanded_conv_depthwise_BN[0][0]
expanded_conv_ project (Conv2D) [0]	(None, 64, 64, 16)	512	expanded_conv_depthwise_relu[0]
expanded_conv_ project_BN (Batch	(None, 64, 64, 16)	64	expanded_conv_project[0][0]
block_1_expand (Conv2D)	(None, 64, 64, 96)	1536	expanded_conv_project_BN[0][0]
block_1_expand_BN (BatchNormali	(None, 64, 64, 96)	384	block_1_expand[0][0]
block_1_expand_ relu (ReLU)	(None, 64, 64, 96)	0	block_1_expand_BN[0][0]
block_1_pad (ZeroPadding2D)	(None, 65, 65, 96)	0	block_1_expand_relu[0][0]
block_1_depthwise (DepthwiseCon	(None, 32, 32, 96)	864	block_1_pad[0][0]
block_1_depthwise _BN (BatchNorm	(None, 32, 32, 96)	384	block_1_depthwise[0][0]
block_1_depthwise_ relu (ReLU)	(None, 32, 32, 96)	0	block_1_depthwise_BN[0][0]
block_1_project (Conv2D)	(None, 32, 32, 24)	2304	block_1_depthwise_relu[0][0]
block_1_project_ BN (BatchNormal	(None, 32, 32, 24)	96	block_1_project[0][0]
block_2_expand (Conv2D)	(None, 32, 32, 144)	3456	block_1_project_BN[0][0]
block_2_expand_ BN (BatchNormali	(None, 32, 32, 144)	576	block_2_expand[0][0]
block_2_expand_ relu (ReLU)	(None, 32, 32, 144)	0	block_2_expand_BN[0][0]
block_2_depthwise (DepthwiseCon	(None, 32, 32, 144)	1296	block_2_expand_relu[0][0]
block_2_depthwise_ BN (BatchNorm	(None, 32, 32, 144)	576	block_2_depthwise[0][0]
block_2_depthwise_ relu (ReLU)	(None, 32, 32, 144)	0	block_2_depthwise_BN[0][0]
block_2_project (Conv2D)	(None, 32, 32, 24)	3456	block_2_depthwise_relu[0][0]

block_2_project_ BN (BatchNormal	(None, 32, 32, 24)	96	block_2_project[0][0]
block_2_add (Add)	(None, 32, 32, 24)	0	block_1_project_BN[0][0] block_2_project_ BN[0][0]
block_3_expand (Conv2D)	(None, 32, 32, 144)	3456	block_2_add[0][0]
block_3_expand_BN (BatchNormali	(None, 32, 32, 144)	576	block_3_expand[0][0]
block_3_expand_ relu (ReLU)	(None, 32, 32, 144)	0	block_3_expand_BN[0][0]
block_3_pad (ZeroPadding2D)	(None, 33, 33, 144)	0	block_3_expand_relu[0][0]
block_3_depthwise (DepthwiseCon	(None, 16, 16, 144)	1296	block_3_pad[0][0]
block_3_depthwise_ BN (BatchNorm	(None, 16, 16, 144)	576	block_3_depthwise[0][0]
block_3_depthwise_ relu (ReLU)	(None, 16, 16, 144)	0	block_3_depthwise_BN[0][0]
block_3_project (Conv2D)	(None, 16, 16, 32)	4608	block_3_depthwise_relu[0][0]
block_3_project_BN (BatchNormal	(None, 16, 16, 32)	128	block_3_project[0][0]
block_4_expand (Conv2D)	(None, 16, 16, 192)	6144	block_3_project_BN[0][0]
block_4_expand_BN (BatchNormali	(None, 16, 16, 192)	768	block_4_expand[0][0]
block_4_expand_ relu (ReLU)	None, 16, 16, 192)	0	block_4_expand_BN[0][0]
block_4_depthwise (DepthwiseCon	(None, 16, 16, 192)	1728	block_4_expand_relu[0][0]
block_4_depthwise_ BN (BatchNorm	(None, 16, 16, 192)	768	block_4_depthwise[0][0]
block_4_depthwise_ relu (ReLU)	(None, 16, 16, 192)	0	block_4_depthwise_BN[0][0]
block_4_project (Conv2D)	(None, 16, 16, 32)	6144	block_4_depthwise_relu[0][0]
block_4_project_ BN (BatchNormal	(None, 16, 16, 32)	128	block_4_project[0][0]
block_4_add (Add)	(None, 16, 16, 32)	0	block_3_project_BN[0][0] block_4_project_ BN[0][0]

block_5_expand (Conv2D)	(None, 16, 16, 192)	6144	block_4_add[0][0]
block_5_expand_BN (BatchNormali	(None, 16, 16, 192)	768	block_5_expand[0][0]
block_5_expand_ relu (ReLU)	(None, 16, 16, 192)	0	block_5_expand_BN[0][0]
block_5_depthwise (DepthwiseCon	(None, 16, 16, 192)	1728	block_5_expand_relu[0][0]
block_5_depthwise_ BN (BatchNorm	(None, 16, 16, 192)	768	block_5_depthwise[0][0]
block_5_depthwise_ relu (ReLU)	(None, 16, 16, 192)	0	block_5_depthwise_BN[0][0]
block_5_project (Conv2D)	(None, 16, 16, 32)	6144	block_5_depthwise_relu[0][0]
block_5_project_ BN (BatchNormal	(None, 16, 16, 32)	128	block_5_project[0][0]
block_5_add (Add) block_5_project_ BN[0][0]	(None, 16, 16, 32)	0	block_4_add[0][0]
block_6_expand (Conv2D)	(None, 16, 16, 192)	6144	block_5_add[0][0]
block_6_expand_ BN (BatchNormali	(None, 16, 16, 192)	768	block_6_expand[0][0]
block_6_expand_ relu (ReLU)	(None, 16, 16, 192)	0	block_6_expand_BN[0][0]
block_6_pad (ZeroPadding2D)	(None, 17, 17, 192)	0	block_6_expand_relu[0][0]
block_6_depthwise (DepthwiseCon	(None, 8, 8, 192)	1728	block_6_pad[0][0]
block_6_depthwise_ BN (BatchNorm	(None, 8, 8, 192)	768	block_6_depthwise[0][0]
block_6_depthwise_ relu (ReLU)	(None, 8, 8, 192)	0	block_6_depthwise_BN[0][0]
block_6_project (Conv2D)	(None, 8, 8, 64)	12288	block_6_depthwise_relu[0][0]
block_6_project_ BN (BatchNormal	(None, 8, 8, 64)	256	block_6_project[0][0]
block_7_expand (Conv2D)	(None, 8, 8, 384)	24576	block_6_project_BN[0][0]
block_7_expand_BN (BatchNormali	(None, 8, 8, 384)	1536	block_7_expand[0][0]

block_7_expand_ relu (ReLU)	(None, 8, 8, 384)	0	block_7_expand_BN[0][0]
block_7_depthwise (DepthwiseCon	(None, 8, 8, 384)	3456	block_7_expand_relu[0][0]
block_7_depthwise_ BN (BatchNorm	(None, 8, 8, 384)	1536	block_7_depthwise[0][0]
block_7_depthwise_ relu (ReLU)	(None, 8, 8, 384)	0	block_7_depthwise_BN[0][0]
block_7_project (Conv2D)	(None, 8, 8, 64)	24576	block_7_depthwise_relu[0][0]
block_7_project_ BN (BatchNormal	(None, 8, 8, 64)	256	block_7_project[0][0]
block_7_add (Add)	(None, 8, 8, 64)	0	block_6_project_BN[0][0] block_7_project_ BN[0][0]
block_8_expand (Conv2D)	(None, 8, 8, 384)	24576	block_7_add[0][0]
block_8_expand_ BN (BatchNormali	(None, 8, 8, 384)	1536	block_8_expand[0][0]
block_8_expand_ relu (ReLU)	(None, 8, 8, 384)	0	block_8_expand_BN[0][0]
block_8_depthwise (DepthwiseCon	(None, 8, 8, 384)	3456	block_8_expand_relu[0][0]
block_8_depthwise_ BN (BatchNorm	(None, 8, 8, 384)	1536	block_8_depthwise[0][0]
block_8_depthwise_ relu (ReLU)	(None, 8, 8, 384)	0	block_8_depthwise_BN[0][0]
block_8_project (Conv2D)	(None, 8, 8, 64)	24576	block_8_depthwise_relu[0][0]
block_8_project_ BN (BatchNormal	(None, 8, 8, 64)	256	block_8_project[0][0]
block_8_add (Add)	(None, 8, 8, 64)	0	block_7_add[0][0] block_8_project_ BN[0][0]
block_9_expand (Conv2D)	(None, 8, 8, 384)	24576	block_8_add[0][0]
block_9_expand_ BN (BatchNormali	(None, 8, 8, 384)	1536	block_9_expand[0][0]
block_9_expand_ relu (ReLU)	(None, 8, 8, 384)	0	block_9_expand_BN[0][0]
block_9_depthwise (DepthwiseCon	(None, 8, 8, 384)	3456	block_9_expand_relu[0][0]

block_9_depthwise_ BN (BatchNorm	(None, 8, 8, 384)	1536	block_9_depthwise[0][0]
block_9_depthwise_ relu (ReLU)	(None, 8, 8, 384)	0	block_9_depthwise_BN[0][0]
block_9_project (Conv2D)	(None, 8, 8, 64)	24576	block_9_depthwise_relu[0][0]
block_9_project_ BN (BatchNormal	(None, 8, 8, 64)	256	block_9_project[0][0]
block_9_add (Add)	(None, 8, 8, 64)	0	block_8_add[0][0] block_9_project_ BN[0][0]
block_10_expand (Conv2D)	(None, 8, 8, 384)	24576	block_9_add[0][0]
block_10_expand_ BN (BatchNormal	(None, 8, 8, 384)	1536	block_10_expand[0][0]
block_10_expand_ relu (ReLU)	(None, 8, 8, 384)	0	block_10_expand_BN[0][0]
block_10_depthwise (DepthwiseCo	(None, 8, 8, 384)	3456	block_10_expand_relu[0][0]
block_10_depthwise_ BN (BatchNor	(None, 8, 8, 384)	1536	block_10_depthwise[0][0]
block_10_depthwise_ relu (ReLU)	(None, 8, 8, 384)	0	block_10_depthwise_BN[0][0]
block_10_project (Conv2D)	(None, 8, 8, 96)	36864	block_10_depthwise_relu[0][0]
block_10_project_ BN (BatchNorma	(None, 8, 8, 96)	384	block_10_project[0][0]
block_11_expand (Conv2D)	(None, 8, 8, 576)	55296	block_10_project_BN[0][0]
block_11_expand_ BN (BatchNormal	(None, 8, 8, 576)	2304	block_11_expand[0][0]
block_11_expand_ relu (ReLU)	(None, 8, 8, 576)	0	block_11_expand_BN[0][0]
block_11_depthwise (DepthwiseCo	(None, 8, 8, 576)	5184	block_11_expand_relu[0][0]
block_11_depthwise_ BN (BatchNor	(None, 8, 8, 576)	2304	block_11_depthwise[0][0]
block_11_depthwise_ relu (ReLU)	(None, 8, 8, 576)	0	block_11_depthwise_BN[0][0]
block_11_project (Conv2D)	(None, 8, 8, 96)	55296	block_11_depthwise_relu[0][0]

block_11_project_ BN (BatchNorma	(None, 8, 8, 96)	384	block_11_project[0][0]
block_11_add (Add) block_11_project_ BN[0][0]	(None, 8, 8, 96)	0	block_10_project_BN[0][0]
block_12_expand (Conv2D)	(None, 8, 8, 576)	55296	block_11_add[0][0]
block_12_expand_ BN (BatchNormal	(None, 8, 8, 576)	2304	block_12_expand[0][0]
block_12_expand_ relu (ReLU)	(None, 8, 8, 576)	0	block_12_expand_BN[0][0]
block_12_depthwise (DepthwiseCo	(None, 8, 8, 576)	5184	block_12_expand_relu[0][0]
block_12_depthwise_ BN (BatchNor	(None, 8, 8, 576)	2304	block_12_depthwise[0][0]
block_12_depthwise_ relu (ReLU)	(None, 8, 8, 576)	0	block_12_depthwise_BN[0][0]
block_12_project (Conv2D)	(None, 8, 8, 96)	55296	block_12_depthwise_relu[0][0]
block_12_project_ BN (BatchNorma	(None, 8, 8, 96)	384	block_12_project[0][0]
block_12_add (Add) block_12_project_ BN[0][0]	(None, 8, 8, 96)	0	block_11_add[0][0]
block_13_expand (Conv2D)	(None, 8, 8, 576)	55296	block_12_add[0][0]
block_13_expand_BN (BatchNormal	(None, 8, 8, 576)	2304	block_13_expand[0][0]
block_13_expand_ relu (ReLU)	(None, 8, 8, 576)	0	block_13_expand_BN[0][0]
block_13_pad (ZeroPadding2D)	(None, 9, 9, 576)	0	block_13_expand_relu[0][0]
block_13_depthwise (DepthwiseCo	(None, 4, 4, 576)	5184	block_13_pad[0][0]
block_13_depthwise_ BN (BatchNor	(None, 4, 4, 576)	2304	block_13_depthwise[0][0]
block_13_depthwise_ relu (ReLU)	(None, 4, 4, 576)	0	block_13_depthwise_BN[0][0]
block_13_project (Conv2D)	(None, 4, 4, 160)	92160	block_13_depthwise_relu[0][0]
block_13_project_ BN (BatchNorma	(None, 4, 4, 160)	640	block_13_project[0][0]

block_14_expand (Conv2D)	(None, 4, 4, 960)	153600	block_13_project_BN[0][0]
block_14_expand_ BN (BatchNormal	(None, 4, 4, 960)	3840	block_14_expand[0][0]
block_14_expand_ relu (ReLU)	(None, 4, 4, 960)	0	block_14_expand_BN[0][0]
block_14_depthwise (DepthwiseCo	(None, 4, 4, 960)	8640	block_14_expand_relu[0][0]
block_14_depthwise_ BN (BatchNor	(None, 4, 4, 960)	3840	block_14_depthwise[0][0]
block_14_depthwise_ relu (ReLU)	(None, 4, 4, 960)	0	block_14_depthwise_BN[0][0]
block_14_project (Conv2D)	(None, 4, 4, 160)	153600	block_14_depthwise_relu[0][0]
block_14_project_ BN (BatchNorma	(None, 4, 4, 160)	640	block_14_project[0][0]
block_14_add (Add)	(None, 4, 4, 160)	0	block_13_project_BN[0][0] block_14_project_ BN[0][0]
block_15_expand (Conv2D)	(None, 4, 4, 960)	153600	block_14_add[0][0]
block_15_expand_ BN (BatchNormal	(None, 4, 4, 960)	3840	block_15_expand[0][0]
block_15_expand_ relu (ReLU)	(None, 4, 4, 960)	0	block_15_expand_BN[0][0]
block_15_depthwise (DepthwiseCo	(None, 4, 4, 960)	8640	block_15_expand_relu[0][0]
block_15_depthwise_ BN (BatchNor	(None, 4, 4, 960)	3840	block_15_depthwise[0][0]
block_15_depthwise_ relu (ReLU)	(None, 4, 4, 960)	0	block_15_depthwise_BN[0][0]
block_15_project (Conv2D)	(None, 4, 4, 160)	153600	block_15_depthwise_relu[0][0]
block_15_project_ BN (BatchNorma	(None, 4, 4, 160)	640	block_15_project[0][0]
block_15_add (Add)	(None, 4, 4, 160)	0	block_14_add[0][0] block_15_project_ BN[0][0]
block_16_expand (Conv2D)	(None, 4, 4, 960)	153600	block_15_add[0][0]
block_16_expand_ BN (BatchNormal	(None, 4, 4, 960)	3840	block_16_expand[0][0]

```
block_16_expand_
relu (ReLU)          (None, 4, 4, 960)   0       block_16_expand_BN[0][0]
─────────────────────────────────────────────────────────────────────────
block_16_depthwise
(DepthwiseCo          (None, 4, 4, 960)   8640    block_16_expand_relu[0][0]
─────────────────────────────────────────────────────────────────────────
block_16_depthwise_
BN (BatchNor          (None, 4, 4, 960)   3840    block_16_depthwise[0][0]
─────────────────────────────────────────────────────────────────────────
block_16_depthwise_
relu (ReLU)          (None, 4, 4, 960)   0       block_16_depthwise_BN[0][0]
─────────────────────────────────────────────────────────────────────────
block_16_project
(Conv2D)             (None, 4, 4, 320)   307200  block_16_depthwise_relu[0][0]
─────────────────────────────────────────────────────────────────────────
block_16_project_
BN (BatchNorma       (None, 4, 4, 320)   1280    block_16_project[0][0]
─────────────────────────────────────────────────────────────────────────
Conv_1 (Conv2D)      (None, 4, 4, 1280)  409600  block_16_project_BN[0][0]
─────────────────────────────────────────────────────────────────────────
Conv_1_bn
(BatchNormalization) (None, 4, 4, 1280)  5120    Conv_1[0][0]
─────────────────────────────────────────────────────────────────────────
out_relu (ReLU)      (None, 4, 4, 1280)  0       Conv_1_bn[0][0]
===========================================================================
Total params: 2,257,984
Trainable params: 412,800
Non-trainable params: 1,845,184
```

6.6.5 Train the Model

Now, we can train the model, using the train data and setting up the parameters like an optimizer, loss function, and metric accuracy.

```
#define the model parameters and train it
model = unet_model(OUTPUT_CHANNELS)
model.compile(optimizer= 'adam', loss=tf.keras.losses.Spa
rseCategoricalCrossentropy(from _ logits=True),metrics=['
accuracy'])
```

6.6.6 Test the Model

We test the model in two stages. In the first stage, as you can see in Figures 6.19 and 6.20, the output is not very clear in one epoch, but after 3000 epoch, the network's output is acceptable and is very close to the true masked image.

```
#test the model using the test data
def create_mask(pred_mask):
  pred_mask = tf.argmax(pred_mask, axis=-1)
```

```
    pred_mask = pred_mask[..., tf.newaxis]
    return pred_mask[0]
def show_predictions(dataset=None, num=1):
  if dataset:
    for image, mask in dataset.take(num):
      pred_mask = model.predict(image)
      display([image[0], mask[0],
create_mask(pred_mask)])
  else:
    display([sample_image, sample_mask,
            create_mask(model.predict(sample_
image[tf.newaxis, ...]))])
show_predictions()


EPOCHS =  25
VAL_SUBSPLITS = 5
VALIDATION_STEPS = info.splits['test'].num_examples//
BATCH_SIZE//VAL_SUBSPLITS
model_history = model.fit(train_dataset,
epochs=EPOCHS,
                steps_per_epoch=STEPS_PER_EPOCH,
                validation_steps=VALIDATION_STEPS,
                validation_data=test_dataset,
                callbacks=[DisplayCallback()])
```

and for predicted mask after 3000 iteration, we can have a better output.

```
import numpy as np
loss = model_history.history['loss']
val_loss = model_history.history['val_loss']
n=np.shape(loss)
print(n)
m=(np.ones(n)-loss)
epochs = range(EPOCHS)
plt.figure()
plt.plot(epochs, m, 'g', label='accuracy')
plt.title1('accuracy')
plt.xlabel('Epoch')
plt.ylabel('accuracy Value')
plt.ylim([0, 1])
plt.legend()
plt.show()
```

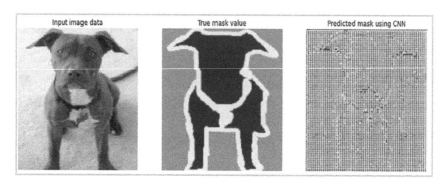

FIGURE 6.19   The predicted mask using CNN after one iteration.

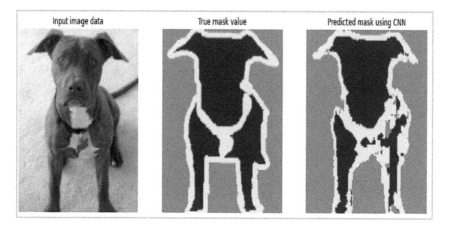

FIGURE 6.20   The predicted mask using CNN after 3000 iterations.

6.7 OBJECT RECOGNITION USING CNNS

Object recognition is a field of image analysis that its goal is to find the object on the images. Humans can easily recognize different objects on an image, but it needs many efforts to make the accuracy acceptable for machines.

6.7.1 Import Libraries

Here, we use python, NumPy, matplotlib, and TensorFlow libraries for computation, visualization, and network modeling.

```
from IPython import display
from matplotlib import pyplot as plt
import numpy as np
import os
import pandas as pd
```

```
from skimage.transform import resize
import tarfile
import sys
sys.path.append("..")
import tensorflow as tf
from tensorflow import keras
from tensorflow.keras import activations, layers,
losses, optimizers, regularizers
```

6.7.2 Load the Data and Generate a Dataset

Here load the dataset from a link and then set the size of the data in the dataset.

```
lfw_url = "http://vis-www.cs.umass.edu/lfw/lfw-
deepfunneled.tgz"
lfw_path = "lfw-deepfunneled.tgz"
keras.utils.get_file(lfw_path, lfw_url, cache_dir=".",
cache_subdir="")
print("Extracting images: ", end="")
data = np.float32([ image for image in progress(read_
images(lfw _ path, size _ x=36, size _ y=36), every=200) ])
```

6.7.3 Make the Model

In this step, we create the model by adding convolution layers. There are two functions here, as we discussed the GAN before (the generator and discriminator). The activation function here is ReLU.

6.7.3.1 The Generator Function

At the first create the generator method:

```
CODE_SIZE = 256
def generator():
  model = keras.Sequential()
  model.add(layers.Input(shape=(CODE_SIZE,),
name='code'))
  model.add(layers.Dense(6*6*32, activation='relu'))
  model.add(layers.Reshape((6,6,32)))
  model.add(layers.Conv2DTranspose(128, kernel_size=5,
activation='relu'))
  model.add(layers.Conv2DTranspose(128, kernel_size=3,
activation='relu'))
  model.add(layers.Conv2DTranspose(64, kernel_size=3,
activation='relu'))
```

```
  model.add(layers.UpSampling2D())
  model.add(layers.Conv2DTranspose(64, kernel_size=3,
activation='relu'))
  model.add(layers.Conv2DTranspose(32, kernel_size=3,
activation='relu'))
  model.add(layers.Conv2DTranspose(32, kernel_size=3,
activation='relu'))
  model.add(layers.Conv2DTranspose(3, kernel_size=3))
  return model
```

6.7.3.2 The Discriminator Function

Now create the discriminator method:

```
def discriminator():
  model = keras.Sequential()
  model.add(layers.Input(shape=IMAGE_SHAPE,
name="image"))
  model.add(layers.Conv2D(32, kernel_size=3,
activation='elu'))
  model.add(layers.Conv2D(32, kernel_size=5,
activation='elu'))
  model.add(layers.Conv2D(64, kernel_size=3,
activation='elu'))
  model.add(layers.MaxPool2D())
  model.add(layers.Conv2D(64, kernel_size=3,
activation='elu'))
  model.add(layers.Conv2D(128, kernel_size=5,
activation='elu'))
  model.add(layers.Conv2D(128, kernel_size=3,
activation='elu'))
  model.add(layers.Flatten())
  model.add(layers.Dense(256, activation='tanh',
kernel_regularizer=regularizers.l2()))
  model.add(layers.Dense(1, activation='sigmoid'))
  return model
```

Now, you can call the generator and check the model summary.

```
keras.backend.clear_session()
gen = generator()
gen.summary()
print("Inputs :", gen.inputs)
print("Outputs:", gen.outputs)
```

```
assert gen.output _ shape[1:] == IMAGE _ SHAPE,
"generator must output an image of shape %s,
but instead it produces %s"%(IMAGE _ SHAPE,gen.
output _ shape[1:])
```

The model summary here shows you the layers and the parameters (trainable and non-trainable) and the total parameters of the network.

Model: "sequential"

Layer (type)	Output Shape	Param #
dense (Dense)	(None, 1152)	296064
reshape (Reshape)	(None, 6, 6, 32)	0
conv2d_transpose (Conv2DTran	(None, 10, 10, 128)	102528
conv2d_transpose_1 (Conv2DTr	(None, 12, 12, 128)	147584
conv2d_transpose_2 (Conv2DTr	(None, 14, 14, 64)	73792
up_sampling2d (UpSampling2D)	(None, 28, 28, 64)	0
conv2d_transpose_3 (Conv2DTr	(None, 30, 30, 64)	36928
conv2d_transpose_4 (Conv2DTr	(None, 32, 32, 32)	18464
conv2d_transpose_5 (Conv2DTr	(None, 34, 34, 32)	9248
conv2d_transpose_6 (Conv2DTr	(None, 36, 36, 3)	867

```
Total params: 685,475
Trainable params: 685,475
Non-trainable params: 0
```

Now call the discriminator function and then check the model summary.

```
disc = discriminator()
disc.summary()
print("Inputs :", disc.inputs)
print("Outputs:", disc.outputs)
```

The model summary and the network structure are as follows.

```
Model: "sequential_1"
```

Layer (type)	Output Shape	Param #
conv2d (Conv2D)	(None, 34, 34, 32)	896
conv2d_1 (Conv2D)	(None, 30, 30, 32)	25632
conv2d_2 (Conv2D)	(None, 28, 28, 64)	18496
max_pooling2d (MaxPooling2D)	(None, 14, 14, 64)	0
conv2d_3 (Conv2D)	(None, 12, 12, 64)	36928
conv2d_4 (Conv2D)	(None, 8, 8, 128)	204928
conv2d_5 (Conv2D)	(None, 6, 6, 128)	147584
flatten (Flatten)	(None, 4608)	0
dense_1 (Dense)	(None, 256)	1179904
dense_2 (Dense)	(None, 1)	257

```
Total params: 1,614,625
Trainable params: 1,614,625
Non-trainable params: 0
```

6.7.4 Train the Model

We can train the model in this step.

```
epoch = tf.Variable(0)
ckpt = tf.train.Checkpoint(epoch=epoch, disc=disc,
gen=gen, disc_opt=disc_opt, gen_opt=gen_opt)
```

```
manager = tf.train.CheckpointManager(ckpt,
directory="./checkpoints", max_to_keep=10)

status = ckpt.restore(manager.latest _ checkpoint)
```

6.7.5 Generate Images

We can generate the image in this step. Figure 6.21 shows the image examples that the network has generated. More epochs generate the better results.

```
for _ in progress(range(30000)):
    codes = sample_codes(100)
    images = sample_images(100)
    for n in range(5):
        disc_opt.minimize(lambda: disc_loss(images,
codes), disc.trainable_weights)
    gen_opt.minimize(lambda: gen_loss(codes), gen.
trainable_weights)
    if epoch.numpy() % 100 == 0:
        display.clear_output(wait=True)
        print("Epoch:", epoch.numpy())
        plot_images(2, 3)
        plot_probas(1000)
        manager.save()
    epoch.assign _ add(1)
```

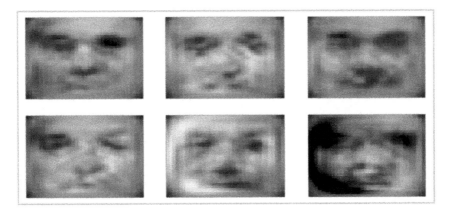

FIGURE 6.21 The generated face using GAN.

## CHAPTER 7

Deep Neural Networks (DNNs) for Virtual Assistant Robots

7.1 VIRTUAL ASSISTANT ROBOT

This chapter presents a project that includes four different types of deep learning applications. This project's goal is to implement a virtual assistant robot that helps experts in the healthcare environment. Assistant robots in the healthcare industry provide a range of essential services, including delivering items (e.g., food, medicine) to users (including clinicians, patients, and visitors), performing precise or dangerous surgeries, alerting nurses to medical emergencies disinfecting tools, and patient rooms. By disinfecting patient rooms and all tools in the rooms, they reduce the risks of contamination or contracting diseases. Also, deploying these robots makes medical tasks more accurate and safer for patients and reduces overall healthcare costs. This chapter discusses and presents problem details, parameters, steps, and some coding sections. The project has four modules:

1. facial detection and recognition,

2. emotion recognition using speech,

3. speech to text, and

4. sentiment analysis.

DOI: 10.1201/9781003025818-7

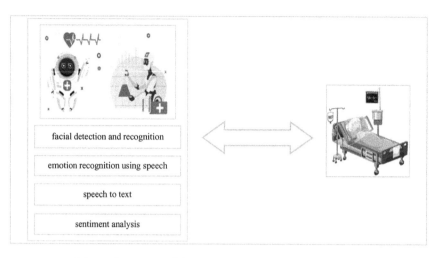

FIGURE 7.1   The architecture of the project.

Figure 7.1 shows the general architecture of the project. The virtual robot gets audio and visual data through the camera and microphone and interacts with the user.

7.2 FACIAL DETECTION AND RECOGNITION

7.2.1 Architecture

There are several research methods for detecting a face in an image and recognizing it. The idea for face recognition is finding the similarities between encoding image vectors (converting each image to one vector of numbers (encoding)). It means, if you pass two images from the same person, the output vectors should be very similar, and if you pass two different person's images, the output vectors should be different. There are several deep learning models for face recognition like DeepFace, VGGFace, and Face Net (Figure 7.2). In addition, you can find five main steps for implementing a face recognition system using deep learning:

Step 1: face detection,

Step 2: landmark detection,

Step 3: encoding the face,

Step 4: loss function, and

Step 5: face matching (recognition).

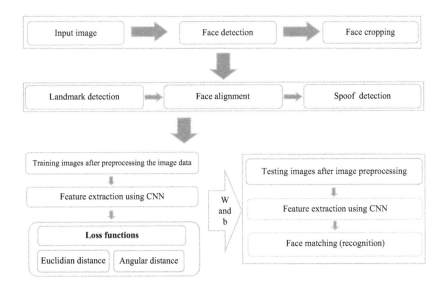

FIGURE 7.2   Facial recognition steps using deep learning.

7.2.2 Face Detection

In the first step, the face should be detected in the context by using a face detection algorithm. One of the facial detection algorithms is the Viola-Jones that use Haar's signs (a set of black and white rectangular filters to move over the images and find the most similar segments to the black or white parts). This section presents the steps and code samples for implementing facial detection using the CNN model (Figure 7.3).

7.2.2.1 Import Libraries

Importing some libraries to ease the computation and plotting. The main libraries are TensorFlow, matplotlib, and NumPy, which help in creating a network, plotting, and computing.

```
import TensorFlow as ft
import matplotlib.pyplot as plt
import NumPy as np
tf.enable_eager_execution()
import functools
```

FIGURE 7.3   Face detection using CNN.

7.2.2.2 Dataset

In this step, choose a database (there are many databases for this purpose) to create training, validation, and testing data. Then, you can use Keras libraries to import and create data segments.

```
Import keras
training _ data = tf.keras.utils.get _ file(…)
```

7.2.2.3 Define CNN Model and Training

Define a CNN model using Keras and determine:

- parameters like the number of the layers,

- hyperparameters like dropout value or activation (transition) function, and

- each layer's features like kernel size and stride size.

Here is the code for defining a CNN model using TensorFlow and Keras:

```
def classifier ():
 Conv2D = functools.partial (tf.keras.layers.Conv2D,
 padding = 'same', activation = 'relu')
 BatchNormalization = tf.keras.layers.
 BatchNormalization
 Flatten = tf.keras.layers.Flatten
 Dense = functools.partial (tf.keras.layers.Dense,
 activation='relu')
 model = tf.keras.Sequential
      ([Conv2D (filters = 1*n_filters, kernel_size =
       [5,5], strides = [1,1]), BatchNormalization(),
       Conv2D (filters = 2*n _ filters, kernel _ size =
       [5, 5], strides = [1, 1]), BatchNormalization(),
       Conv2D (filters = 4*n _ filters, kernel _ size =
       [3, 3], strides = [1, 1]), BatchNormalization(),
       Conv2D (filters = 6*n _ filters, kernel _ size =
       [3, 3], strides = [1, 1]), BatchNormalization(),
       Flatten (), Dense (1, activation=None),
       tf.keras.layers.Dropout (0.5)])
  return model
```

7.2.2.4 Model Training

Train the model by defining some parameters like batch normalization size, number of epochs, and learning rate. After loading the training images, convert them to the tensors and then do training as follows:

```
batch_size = 24
num_epochs = 100
learning_rate = 1e-2
# optimizer definition
optimizer = tf.train.AdamOptimizer (learning_rate =
learning_rate)
# the loss definition
loss_history = util.LossHistory (smoothing_factor =
0.99)
# the training loop!
for epoch in range (num_epochs):
        custom_msg = util.custom_progress_text ("Epoch:
        %(epoch).0f Loss: %(loss)2.2f")
        bar = util.create_progress_bar (custom_msg)
 for idx in bar (range (loader.get_train_size ())//
batch_size)):
# convert the images to tensors
        x, y = loader.get_batch (batch_size)
        x = tf.convert_to_tensor (x, dtype=tf.float32)
        y = tf.convert_to_tensor (y, dtype=tf.float32)
    with tf.GradientTape () as tape:
     logits = standard_classifier (x)
      # compute the loss
       loss_value = tf.nn.sigmoid_cross_entropy_with_
       logits(labels = y, logits = logits)
      custom_msg.update_mapping(epoch = epoch, loss =
      loss_value.numpy().mean())
      # backpropagation
      grads = tape.gradient(loss_value, standard_
      classifier.variables)
      optimizer.apply_gradients (zip(grads,standard_
      classifier.variables) global_step = tf.train.
      get_or_create_global_step())
      loss_history.append(loss_value.numpy().mean())
      return loss _ history.get()
```

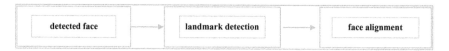

FIGURE 7.4   Landmark detection.

7.2.2.5 Evaluate Performance
Evaluate the performance of the model by using validation data.

```
# Evaluate on a subset of dataset
(batch_x, batch_y) = loader.get_batch(5000)
y_pred_standard = tf.round(tf.nn.sigmoid(standard_
classifier.predict(batch_x)))
acc _ standard = tf.reduce _ mean(tf.cast(tf.
equal(batch _ y, y _ pred _ standard), tf.float32))
```

7.2.3 Landmark Detection
In this step, the algorithm finds the face landmarks/poses. It needs these points for face alignment (here, we already collected the data and detected the face) (Figure 7.4).

7.2.3.1 CNN Model
There are different CNN methods for finding the landmarks. VGG-16 is one of the first CNN methods, and here we use its architecture for finding the landmarks.

```
model   =   Sequential()
model.add (Conv2D(filters =16, kernel_size = 3,
activation = 'relu', input_shape = (28, 28, 1)))
model.add (MaxPooling2D(pool_size = 2))
model.add (Conv2D(filters = 32, kernel_size = 3,
activation = 'relu'))
model.add (MaxPooling2D(pool_size = 2))
model.add (Conv2D(filters = 64, kernel_size = 3,
activation = 'relu'))
model.add (MaxPooling2D(pool_size = 2))
model.add (Conv2D(filters = 128, kernel_size = 3,
activation = 'relu'))
model.add (MaxPooling2D(pool_size = 2))
model.add (Conv2D(filters = 256, kernel_size = 3,
activation = 'relu'))
model.add (MaxPooling2D(pool_size = 2))
model.add (Flatten())
model.add (Dense(512, activation = 'relu'))
```

```
model.add (Dropout(0.2))
model.add (Dense(30))
model.summary()
```

The output is the model summary of the network that shows the layers and the parameters.

Layer (type)	Output Shape	Param #
conv2d_70 (Conv2D)	(None, 94, 94, 16)	160
max_pooling2d_62 (MaxPooling)	(None, 47, 47, 16)	0
conv2d_71 (Conv2D)	(None, 45, 45, 32)	4640
max_pooling2d_63 (MaxPooling)	(None, 22, 22, 32)	0
conv2d_72 (Conv2D)	(None, 20, 20, 64)	18496
max_pooling2d_64 (MaxPooling)	(None, 10, 10, 64)	0
conv2d_73 (Conv2D)	(None, 8, 8, 128)	73856
max_pooling2d_65 (MaxPooling)	(None, 4, 4, 128)	0
conv2d_74 (Conv2D)	(None, 2, 2, 256)	295168
max_pooling2d_66 (MaxPooling)	(None, 1, 1, 256)	0
flatten_5 (Flatten)	(None, 256)	0
dense_10 (Dense)	(None, 512)	131584
dropout_5 (Dropout)	(None, 512)	0
dense_11 (Dense)	(None, 30)	15390

```
Total params: 539, 294
Trainable params: 539, 294
Non-trainable params: 0
```

7.2.3.2 Model Training

Now compile and train the model:

```
epochs = 10
batch_size = 32
filepath = 'model_weights.ckpt'
checkpointer = ModelCheckpoint(filepath, verbose =1,
save_best_only = True, period = 5)
#Compile the model
model.compile(optimizer = 'adam', loss = 'mse',
metrics = ['accuracy'])
history = model.fit(train_input, train_output,
validation_split = 0.2, callbacks =
[checkpointer,hist], batch_size = batch_size, epochs =
epochs, verbose=1)
model.save('my _ model.h5')
```

7.2.3.3 Test the Trained Model

You can use the testing data to evaluate the model performance.

```
print("Test data shape == {}".format(X_test.shape))
predictions = model.predict(X_test)
fig = plt.figure(figsize = (6, 6))
fig.subplots_adjust(left = 0, right = 1, bottom = 0,
top = 1, hspace = 0.05, wspace = 0.05)
for i in range(4):
    ax = fig.add_subplot(2, 2, i + 1, xticks = [],
    yticks =[])
    plotData(X _ test[i], predictions[i], ax)
```

7.2.4 Spoof Detection

Anti-spoofing is a very important step in facial recognition. For example, people can use the photo of a person to access his/her account, and it is a real problem in the real-world problems that deploy facial recognition systems for their security. For this purpose, there are different methods. One of these methods is using infrared (IR) sensors. Also, you can use deep learning for this purpose. You can deploy the VGG-16 architecture (the same as the previous section here). You can create a supervised or unsupervised method for detecting the live images for training the model (depend on the live and fake image data that you have (supervised) or if you don't have enough data for training(unsupervised)). In real-time problems, using IR gives you a real-time response (Figure 7.5).

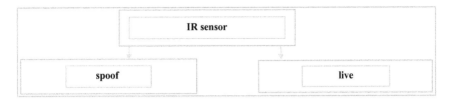

FIGURE 7.5   Spoof detection using IR.

FIGURE 7.6   Encoding the face.

7.2.5 Encoding the Face

Using the real face data from the previous step, you can find the encoding vector for each face. In this step, the face images will transfer to the CNN (or deep learning model). Each detected face image is converted to a vector, and then these vectors are feed to the network for training (Figure 7.6).

7.2.6 Training

After extracting the features in the training step, the loss function like Euclidean distance or angular distance extracts the final trained model. The most popular loss function is Euclidean distance (Figure 7.7).

7.2.7 Testing

After the feature extraction on the test images, the algorithm uses some threshold comparison and metric learning to do the face matching. These techniques compare the encoding vectors from the training database with the encoding vectors from faces in the test database to recognize the person. The accuracy can be calculated with a different metric (we discussed before (Figure 7.8)).

FIGURE 7.7   Training to find the model.

FIGURE 7.8   Testing trained model.

7.3 EMOTION RECOGNITION USING SPEECH

Let us see how to deploy deep learning for emotion recognition using audio (speech) data. The output of this step transfers to the next step for sentiment analysis. It would help when you do some preprocessing on the data and then create an initial trained model. After importing the necessary libraries, there are five major steps for creating architecture:

1. dataset collection,

2. data preprocessing,

3. model training,

4. model evaluation, and

5. evaluate the trained model.

7.3.1 Dataset Collection

There are several verified datasets like the RAVDESS (audiovisual dataset). However, if you plan to run a specific project, it is better to collect your own dataset. Depending on the output and the features you plan to classify (your data should have those features), you can decide about the data collection type. For example, there are some criteria like 3D data or indoor and outdoor data for the image (this step extracts the data values). For instance, in the RAVDESS dataset (Figure 7.9), the values are path, actor, gender, intensity, repetition, and emotion states. Here the basic emotion states are happiness, sadness, disgust, anger, calm, fear, surprise, and neutral.

```
data_df = pd.DataFrame (columns = ['path', 'src',
'actor', 'gender','intensity', 'statement',
'repetition', 'emotion'])
count = 0
```

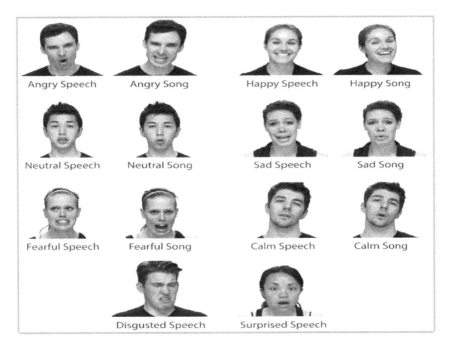

FIGURE 7.9.　RAVDESS dataset data sample.

```
for i in dir_list1:
    file_list = os.listdir('path' + i)
    for f in file_list:
        nm = f.split('.')[0].split('-')
        path = 'path' + i + '/' + f
        if int(actor)%2 == 0:
            gender = "female"
        else:
            gender = "male"
src = int(nm[1])
emotion = int(nm[2])
if nm[3] == '01':
            intensity = 0
  else:
            intensity = 1
  if nm[4] == '01':
            statement = 0
  else:
            statement = 1
  if nm[5] == '01':
            repeat = 0
```

```
    else:
              repeat = 1
      actor = int(nm[6])
data_df.loc[count] = [path, src, actor, gender,
intensity, statement, repeat, emotion]
    count += 1
```

7.3.2 Data Preprocessing

In this step, do some preprocessing on the data to make data ready for training. It may include data cleaning, feature extraction, labeling, and data augmenting.

7.3.2.1 Labeling

If the data are from databases, they are usually annotated and if you plan to collect your data, you should label them. The labeling is depending on the type of the problem and the feature you would like to classify. For example, in this project, the labels are male or females, positive or negative, and there are seven different emotion states:

```
label_list = []
for i in range(len(data_df)):
    if data_df.emotion[i] == 1:
        lb = "_neutral"
    elif data_df.emotion[i] == 2:
        lb = "_calm"
    elif data_df.emotion[i] == 3:
        lb = "_happy"
    elif data_df.emotion[i] == 4:
        lb = "_sad"
    elif data_df.emotion[i] == 5:
        lb = "_angry"
    elif data_df.emotion[i] == 6:
        lb = "_fearful"
    elif data_df.emotion[i] == 7:
        lb = "_disgust"
    elif data_df.emotion[i] == 8:
        lb = "_surprised"
    else:
        lb = "_none"
    label_list.append(data_df.gender[i]  + lb)
```

7.3.3 Feature Extraction

For training, extract some audio features that make the differences between sounds. The raw data in audio are in the time domain, and with some functions like FFT, you can transfer them to the frequency domain. The audio signals have some features like frequency (frequency domain), mel-frequency cepstrum (MFC), or mel-frequency cepstral coefficients (MFCCs) (texture of the sound), which you can extract them to use as a feature vector for training. Standard libraries like librosa help you to do some signal analysis, like loading the data and finding a sample rate:

```
data = pd.DataFrame(columns=['feature'])
for i in tqdm(range(len(data_df))):
    X, sample_rate = librosa.load(data_df.path[i],
res_type = 'kaiser_fast',duration = input_duration,sr
= 22050*2, offset = 0.5)
    sample_rate = np.array(sample_rate)
    mfccs = np.mean(librosa.feature.mfcc(y = X, sr =
sample_rate, n_mfcc = 13), axis = 0)
    feature = mfccs
    data.loc[i] = [feature]
```

7.3.3.1 Data Augmentation

In deep learning, you need a large amount of data to train the model (there are always some limitations for data). You can use data augmentation techniques to generate new data and increase the database size. Here for the audio signals, you can do some tasks like adding noise, shifting time using NumPy, changing pitch, and changing speed using Librosa.

```
def noise(data)
    noise_amp = 0.005*np.random.uniform()*np.
    amax(data)
    data = data.astype('float64') + noise_amp *
    np.random.normal(size = data.shape[0])
    return data
def shift(data):
    s_range = int(np.random.uniform(low = -5, high =
    5)*500)
    return np.roll(data, s_range)
def speedNpitch(data):
    length_change = np.random.uniform(low = 0.8,
    high = 1)
    speed_fac = 1.0  / length_change
```

```
tmp = np.interp(np.arange(0,len(data),speed_
fac),np.arange(0,len(data)),data)
minlen = min(data.shape[0], tmp.shape[0])
data *= 0
data[0:minlen] = tmp[0:minlen]
return data
```

7.3.4 Model Training

In this step, you can define the model and optimizer, for CNN model. Now you can train the model with a part of the dataset (training data about 70 to 80 percent of the original dataset):

```
model = Sequential()
model.add(Conv1D(256, 5, padding = 'same',input_shape
= (X_train.shape[1],1)))
model.add(Activation('relu'))
model.add(Conv1D(256, 5, padding = 'same'))
model.add(BatchNormalization())
model.add(Activation('relu'))
model.add(Dropout(0.25))
model.add(MaxPooling1D(pool_size = (8)))
model.add(Conv1D(128, 5, padding = 'same'))
model.add(Activation('relu'))
model.add(Conv1D(128, 5, padding = 'same'))
model.add(Activation('relu'))
model.add(Conv1D(128, 5, padding = 'same'))
model.add(Activation('relu'))
model.add(Conv1D(128, 5, padding = 'same'))
model.add(BatchNormalization())
model.add(Activation('relu'))
model.add(Dropout(0.25))
model.add(MaxPooling1D(pool_size = (8)))
model.add(Conv1D(64, 5, padding = 'same'))
model.add(Activation('relu'))
model.add(Conv1D(64, 5, padding = 'same'))
model.add(Activation('relu'))
model.add(Flatten())
model.add(Dense(14))
model.add(Activation('softmax'))
opt = keras.optimizers.SGD(lr = 0.0001, momentum = 0.0,
decay = 0.0, nesterov = False)
```

and here is the model summary:

Layer (type)	Output Shape	Param #
conv1d_8 (Conv1D)	(None, 259, 256)	1536
activation_9 (Activation)	(None, 259, 256)	0
conv1d_9 (Conv1D)	(None, 259, 256)	327936
batch_normalization_2 (Batch)	(None, 259, 256)	1024
activation_10 (Activation)	(None, 259, 256)	0
dropout_2 (Dropout)	(None, 259, 256)	0
max_pooling1d_2 (MaxPooling1)	(None, 32, 256	0
conv1d_10 (Conv1D)	(None, 32, 128)	163968
activation_11 (Activation)	(None, 32, 128)	0
conv1d_11 (Conv1D)	(None, 32, 128)	82048
activation_12 (Activation)	(None, 32, 128)	0
conv1d_12 (Conv1D)	(None, 32, 128)	82048
activation_13 (Activation)	(None, 32, 128)	0
conv1d_13 (Conv1D)	(None, 32, 128)	82048
batch_normalization_3 (Batch)	(None, 32, 128)	512
activation_14 (Activation)	(None, 32, 128)	0
dropout_3 (Dropout)	(None, 32, 128)	0
max_pooling1d_3 (MaxPooling1)	(None, 4, 128)	0
conv1d_14 (Conv1D)	(None, 4, 64)	41024

activation_15 (Activation)	(None, 4, 64)	0
conv1d_15 (Conv1D)	(None, 4, 64)	20544
activation_16 (Activation)	(None, 4, 64)	0
flatten_1 (Flatten)	(None, 256)	0
dense_1 (Dense)	(None, 14)	3598
activation_17 (Activation)	(None, 14)	0

```
=========================================================
Total params: 806, 286
Trainable params: 805, 518
Non-trainable params: 768
```

The model should train with the training data:

```
model.compile(loss = 'mean_squared_error', optimizer
= 'sgd', metrics = [metrics.categorical_accuracy])
lr_reduce = ReduceLROnPlateau(monitor = 'val_loss',
factor = 0.9, patience = 20, min_lr = 0.01)
mcp_save = ModelCheckpoint('C:/model/Model.h5', save_
best_only = True, monitor = 'val_loss', mode = 'min')
cnnhistory= model.fit(x _ traincnn, y _ train, batch _
size = 16, epochs = 50,validation _ data = (x _ testcnn,
y _ test), callbacks = [mcp _ save, lr _ reduce])
```

7.3.5 Model Evaluation

Now, you can validate and evaluate your model using the validation and test dataset. You can change different parameters and hyperparameters in the previous steps (1-3) to achieve the desired accuracy, optimize the model, and move to the next step.

```
data_test = pd.DataFrame(columns=['feature'])
for i in tqdm(range(len(data_df))):
    X, sample_rate = librosa.load(data_df.path[i],
    res_type = 'kaiser_fast',duration = input_
    duration,sr = 22050*2,offset = 0.5)
    sample_rate = np.array(sample_rate)
    mfccs = np.mean(librosa.feature.mfcc(y = X, sr =
    sample_rate, n_mfcc = 13), axis = 0)
```

```
    feature = mfccs
    data_test.loc[i] = [feature]
test_valid = pd.DataFrame(data_test['feature'].values.
tolist())
test_valid = np.array(test_valid)
test_valid_lb = np.array(data_df.label)
lb = LabelEncoder()
test_valid_lb = np_utils.to_categorical(lb.
fit_transform(test_valid_lb))
test _ valid = np.expand _ dims(test _ valid, axis=2)
```

7.3.6 Test the Trained Model

After getting the desired accuracy, you can save the trained model for testing with new data.

7.4 SPEECH TO TEXT

You can do the speech-to-text in these steps by using different deep learning models. Here the model input is raw audio data, and the output is the
transcription of the person's spoken data. In this section, some parts like
loading or splitting data have been skipped. There are several databases
that you can use for this purpose. For example, LibriSpeech contains 1000
hours of speech, and the data derived from some audiobooks is one choice.
You can define three main steps here:

Step 1: feature extraction,

Step 2: making the model using a deep learning algorithm, and

Step 3: decoding and find the output.

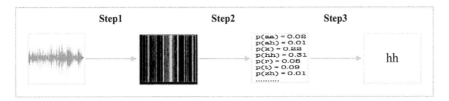

FIGURE 7.9   Speech to text steps.

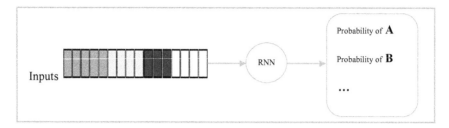

FIGURE 7.10   Shows the RNN architecture.

7.4.1 Feature Extraction

Doing some popular processing on speech to extract the features. Here, we extract two features: spectrograms and MFCC. There are several references if you would like to learn more about these features. Here, the spectrogram function's output is a 2D tensor where the first dimension is the time, and the second dimension is the frequency values. The second feature MFCC has the same concept as the spectrogram, and its feature vector has lower dimensions than the spectrogram. The features here are spectrograms and Mel-Frequency Cepstral Coefficients (MFCCs). Several libraries like librosa (we used in the previous section) can be used here to extract these features.

7.4.2 Deep Neural Networks Modeling

If you know the basic design of a network for acoustic data, you can create your own model for your project. It is sequential, and if we have **n** time slot, every time, the input of the RNN is one of the alphabet characters. There are 28 characters, including 26 letters, a space character (" "), and an apostrophe ('), that every time the speaker pronounces one of these sets. The Figure 7.10 shows an equivalent, rolled depiction of the RNN that shows the output layer in greater detail. The output of the RNN is also a vector that contains the probabilities of all inputs.

7.4.3 Decoder

In this step, the coded data should convert to the original text format coded in the first step. Here is the sample code for the RNN model using Keras.

```
from keras import backend as K
from keras.models import Model
from keras.layers import (BatchNormalization, Conv1D,
Dense, Input, TimeDistributed, Activation,
Bidirectional, SimpleRNN, GRU, LSTM)
```

```
def rnn_model(input_dim, output_dim = 26):
    # Main acoustic input
    input_data = Input(name='the_input', shape =
    (None, input_dim))
    # Add recurrent layer
    simp_rnn = GRU(output_dim, return_sequences =
    True, implementation = 2, name = 'rnn')
    (input_data)
    # Add softmax activation layer
    y_pred = Activation('softmax', name = 'softmax')
    (simp_rnn)
    # Specify the model
    model = Model(inputs = input_data, outputs =
    y_pred)
    model.output_length = lambda x: x
    print(model.summary())
    return model
```

7.4.4 Predictions Calculation

You can write a function to decode the predictions of your acoustic model.

7.5 SENTIMENT ANALYSIS

There are many applications for sentiment analysis. For example, suppose a company created a product, and they would like to know about the user feedback to improve their product. One of the methods is to check customer feedback through social media comments like Twitter and Facebook. For example, if there are thousands of words on customer feedback, doing sentiment analysis helps get a general opinion about the positive or negative of a product. For doing sentiment analysis, you should know about text processing. Text is another type of data (that is the output here). In this step, we use these text data (extracted in the previous step) to do some sentiment analysis to decide or generate a report. You should know two definitions: a) bag of the word: it is a sequence of the word and b) word embedding: it is the process of converting word to vector. If you have a bag of words, using some methods like MLP is not good for this purpose. You can use a deep neural network to convert a sequence of the words to a vector (encoding) and then convert the vector to a sequence of the desired format (decoding). After converting each word to a vector, there is a matrix (each row in this matrix is a vector that represents a word) for a set of the word. Now the algorithm finds the probability of the word's occurrence and the words around this word. Then by using SoftMax, it converts each word value and probabilities to one probability. Each word in the same context has a similar vector. For example, the words kitchen and oven are similar in comparison to kitchen and history.

There are two main parts in DAN:

- **an encoder**: converts the input sequence to a vector depends on the type of coding, and

- **a decoder**: the encoder passes the vector to the decoder, and it converts the vector to the desire outputs.

There are several methods for this purpose, and one of them is the deep averaging network (DAN). This network does word embeddings for all words in the sentence, averaging these vectors (encoding) and then putting them in the network. The network's output is a scalar (decoding) that determines the sentence's value as positive or negative. In DAN, at first, we get a sequence of words and then convert these words to the vectors and then find the average of these vectors and pass this vector to the network and do training by using some methods like Stochastic Gradient Descent (SGD). However, DAN has a problem in the output that it does not do order in the sequence. For example, when the sentence, be: The fire destroyed the houses, maybe the output be: The houses destroyed fire, that the concepts are different. For this purpose, we can use a recurrent neural network.

These are the steps for sentiment analysis using DAN:

1. load dataset,

2. create DAN network,

3. train the network, and

4. evaluate model.

7.5.1 Load Dataset

In this step, load the dataset, put data in the training and testing category, and label them positively and negatively. Create a dictionary of the words for the word embedding process. You need a function to convert the words to the vector. Train and test review can be stored as a data frame and the vocabulary as a dictionary with key (word) and value(index). The vocabulary is used to find a bag of word features.

For example, for negative review and positive review:

```
my_vocab = {'Deep': 0, 'learning': 1, 'in': 2,
'practice': 3}
my_sentence = ' I love to learn deep learning in
practice and do my machine learning project.'
You can create a function to extract the features,
such as the word's occurrence in a sentence.
my_featurs = generate_featur(my_vocab)
the output here should be:
array ([[1, 2, 1, 1]])
```

It means the sentence has **one** deep, **two** learning, **one** in, and **one** practice.

7.5.2 Create a DAN Network

Define two functions:

1. The average function takes tensors as inputs which each one is a bag of the word representation of reviews that its output is tensor for the averaged review.

2. The forward function takes tensor as a bag of word representation of reviews and calls the average function to find the averaged review and send it to the layer to find the model.

7.5.3 Train the Network

In this stage, you can call the DAN network by training data to find the trained network.

7.5.4 Evaluate the Model

Now, you can evaluate your trained model using the test data.

## CHAPTER 8

Finding the Best Model

8.1 DATA PREPROCESSING

The goal of this chapter is to learn how to find the best-trained model with the minimum error. In the first step, let us review the data categories that we need in our projects. In total, we can divide the original data into three categories:

1. training data,

2. validation data, and

3. test data.

We have discussed about these three categories, and you know their definitions. The key point here is the percentage of each category that there are some numbers like 70% for training, 15% for validation, and 15% for testing. If the tested model on the test data reached the desired accuracy, we can utilize it with new real-world data. These ratios are not fixed, and you can change and check the results to find the best percentages. Figure 8.1 shows these three segments.

After the training step and finding the first model using the training data, you can use the validation data to check if the trained model is good for your goal or not. If it is not, you can find the reasons to improve the model. The reasons are directly or indirectly related to several elements like the nature of the data, features of the data, networks parameters, and hyperparameters. The question is, which of these values can make the model less appropriate for our project, and how can we change them?

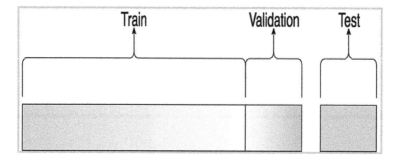

FIGURE 8.1   Split the original data into three parts.

There is a lot of active research in this field, and in this chapter, we discuss and analyze this question and present some solutions for it.

8.2 WHAT IS A GOOD MODEL?

The first step to evaluate the model is calculating the accuracy or finding out the error. When the error is high (accuracy is low), it means the model does not work properly and does not cover the desired goal. There are several methods and measurements to find the accuracy (finding the error). There are two types of errors for checking the model: validation error and test error. For finding out whether a model is good or not, you can work on the validation error. It depends on the data you have and checks how much they are valid to evaluate the model. In the beginning, it is better to check the model with validation error to find the best model for testing using test data. If the validation error is high or does not meet your needs, then the model is not good enough to use. To solve the problem, you should decompose the validation error at the first step:

$$\text{Validation Error} = \text{Noise} + \text{Bias} + \text{Variance}$$

Figure 8.2 shows the validation error segments that calculating these segments is the first step for analyzing the model and evaluating it. In the formula, the variance, bias, and noise can be calculated as follows:

$$\textbf{Variance} = \mathbb{E}\left[\left(h_D(\mathbf{X}) - h^-(\mathbf{X})\right)^2\right]$$

$$\textbf{Bias} = \mathbb{E}\left[\left(h^-(\mathbf{X}) - y^-(\mathbf{X})\right)^2\right]$$

$$\textbf{Noise} = \mathbb{E}\left[\left(y^-(\mathbf{X}) - y^-(\mathbf{X})\right)^2\right]$$

FIGURE 8.2   There are three main parts in error definition.

Now let us put these values in one formula:

$$\mathbb{E}\left[\left(h_D(\mathbf{X})-y\right)^2\right]=\mathbb{E}\left[\left(h_D(\mathbf{X})-\bar{h}(\mathbf{X})\right)^2\right]+\mathbb{E}\left[\left(\bar{h}(\mathbf{X})-\bar{y}(\mathbf{X})\right)^2\right]$$
$$+\mathbb{E}\left[\left(\bar{y}(\mathbf{X})-y(\mathbf{X})\right)^2\right]$$

8.3 WHAT IS THE NOISE?

There is a large amount of meaningless information that makes the data unreliable. This happens because of different reasons like data corruption and the data that users cannot realize or interpret. This information can affect the training process and make the trained model and the results inaccurate. The question is: how can we find the reasons, and what is the solution? And how much it is crucial when the noise is very high, or it has an unacceptable value (please remember that generally, the noise is roughly constant in the problems). In the first step, let us calculate the noise.

For calculating the noise, look at these:

$$\text{Note}=\mathbb{E}\left[\left(y^-(\mathbf{X})-y(\mathbf{X})\right)^2\right]=1/n\left(\sum_{(i=0:m)}\left(y^-(x_i)-y(x_i)\right)^2\right)$$

where:

$$y^-(\mathbf{X})=1*p(y=1|\mathbf{X})+2*p(y=2|\mathbf{X})$$

For better understanding, assume there is a database $\mathbf{D}=\{(\mathbf{x}_1,\mathbf{y}_1),\ldots,(\mathbf{x}_n,\mathbf{y}_n)\}$ with distribution $\mathbf{P(X,Y)}$. Here each pair, $(\mathbf{x}_i,\mathbf{y}_i)$ for $\mathbf{i=1\ldots n}$ is a feature vector for each sample that the $\mathbf{x}_1\ldots\mathbf{x}_n$ are the sample data, and $\mathbf{y}_i$ are the labels.

For example, if the sample is apple, then the x_1 is the first sample, and the y_1 is the value that shows this sample is apple or not. The x_1 is the feature vector that here, for example, is the price, shape, and color (so the x dimension here is 3). The $y^-(x)$ is the expected label, and $y(x)$ is the label, and the $x = \{x_1,...,x_n\}$. Sometimes the noises are on the data, and in this case, you can do some preprocessing on data like noise removal before using data for training. But if you do all the preprocessing and realize the noise value is still high, you should look for some other reasons to reduce the noise or remove it.

Two main reasons that make the noises high are:

- incorrect labeling and
- incorrect feature extraction.

For these two reasons, there are two solutions.

- label the data again and,
- change the features and do the feature extraction.

Remember that the definitions here are for the individual data sample and not about the nature of the data. Figure 8.3 shows the noise on the image data that corrupted the image completely.

FIGURE 8.3 The noise on data can change the results (here, the noise is on the nature of data and can be removed by some preprocesses on data).

8.3.1 Labeling

When the noise is high, then there are possibilities that the labeling is not correct, and you should do labeling again. Let us explain more with an example. If you label some orange data instead of apple, you have incorrectly labeled data that makes the training problematic, like noise data, and made the model inaccurate. For solving this problem, do these steps:

- check the labels,

- find the incorrectly labeled data, and

- relabel data,

- do noise calculation to check the noise value changes.

If you find that the noise has been changed and decreased after the last step, labeling is the main reason; otherwise, we should check other reasons to remove the noise. Figure 8.4 shows how incorrect labeling can be noisy and make the error value high.

8.3.2 Features

Another reason that can make the noise high is incorrect features. For example, if you choose a feature like, apple seed, maybe it is not the correct feature that can help train the model. Also, maybe choosing some features gives a better model compared to others. For example, if you select the color and shape for the object classification problem, maybe the features

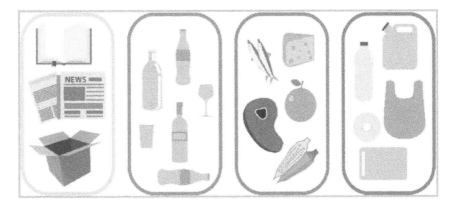

FIGURE 8.4 Incorrect labeling data can make the noise value high (this is the noise we discuss here).

like shape and material can make the data definition more accurate. The key point here is to analyze the problem correctly and determine which features show a better data presentation. For example, for speech data, the Mel frequency and spectrum show the audio data structure better. So, if you realize the noise is high, do these steps:

- check the features,
- analyze the problem again,
- check if the current features can cover your sample definition correctly or not,
- try to find new features,
- change the features vectors,
- training the model using new features, and
- do noise calculations to discover how it changes the noise value.

Now, if the noise has been reduced, it shows the incorrect features are the main reason.

8.4 WHAT IS THE BIAS?

Bias is another part of the error values. We always have a bias data in our dataset. When we are talking about the bias in data, it means that data samples are not all good representations of the total population. When the data are biased, then the information is not reliable to use for training the model. Here, we calculate the bias, analyze it, and find a way to make the data unbiased or less biased. One way to calculate the bias is:

$$|\text{predicted classifier} - \text{average labels}|$$

$$\mathbf{Bias} = \mathbb{E}\left[\left(h^-(\mathbf{X}) - y^-(\mathbf{X})\right)^2\right]$$

Where:

$$h^-(\mathbf{X}) \approx 1/m\left(\sum_{i=1:m} h_{Di}(\mathbf{X})\right)$$

$$y^-(\mathbf{X}) = 1 * p(y = 1|\mathbf{X}) + 2 * p(y = 2|\mathbf{X})$$

Here, **m** is the number of classifiers, $\mathbf{D_i}$ is a dataset, and $\mathbf{h_{Di}}$ is **Di**'s trained classifier. There are several reasons for the high bias in the model. Two main reasons that can bias the information are:

- choosing the incorrect classifier and

- using incorrect features.

There are the same discussion and examples if you choose the incorrect features and how it can affect the inaccurate modeling (Figure 8.5). The $y^-(\mathbf{x})$ is the expected label, and $y(\mathbf{x})$ is the label and the $\mathbf{x} = \{x_1,...,i_n\}$.

8.4.1 Incorrect Classifier

When the bias is high, there is a possibility that the classifier is not correct, and the classifier cannot train data behavior. For example, when you are using linear classifiers for nonlinear data (Figure 8.6).

8.4.2 Incorrect Features

Choosing the correct features is one of the key points in finding the proper model. The features are directly and indirectly effective on the training and the classification results (Figure 8.7).

FIGURE 8.5   High bias can make the results inaccurate.

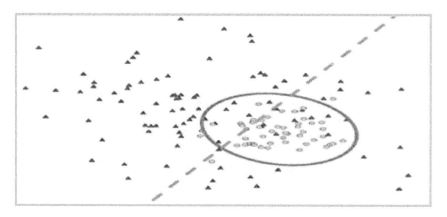

FIGURE 8.6   A correct classifier can make the bias better.

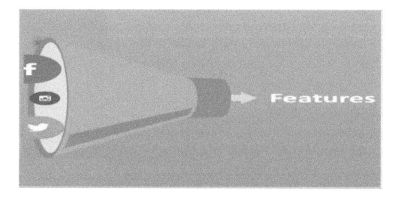

FIGURE 8.7   The wrong feature can make the error high.

8.5 WHAT IS THE VARIANCE?

Variance (σ2) is another part of the error. Variance is a way to measure how far each value of the sample in the data is from the whole dataset's mean value. In general, for its calculation, at first, subtract the mean from each of the sample values, then divide the sum of the squares by the number of sample values in the whole data. Here, we calculate the variance as a part of the error, and then if it is high, it means a big part of the error is because of it, and then try to find ways to reduce it (Figure 8.8). There are some methods for reducing the variance, like bagging or choosing a good dataset. The $y^-(\mathbf{x})$ is the expected label, and $y(\mathbf{x})$ is the label, the

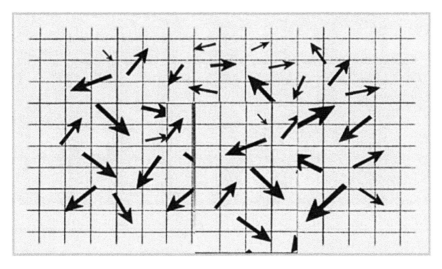

FIGURE 8.8 High variance changes the accuracy.

$\mathbf{x} = \{x_1, \ldots, o_n\}$ and $\mathbf{m}$ is the number of classifiers, $\mathbf{D_i}$ is a dataset, and $\mathbf{h_{Di}}$ is Di's trained classifier. Look at the formula in more detail:

$$\mathbf{Variance} = \mathbb{E}\left[\left(h_D(\mathbf{X}) - h^-(\mathbf{X})\right)^2\right]$$

$$\mathbb{E}_D\left[\left(h_D(\mathbf{X}) - h^-(\mathbf{X})\right)^2\right] \approx 1/m\left(\sum_{i=1:m}\left(h_{Dj}(\mathbf{X_i}) - h^-(\mathbf{X_i})\right)^2\right)$$

Where:

$$h^-(\mathbf{X}) \approx 1/m\left(\sum_{i=1:m}h_{Di}(\mathbf{X})\right)$$

$$y^-(\mathbf{X}) = 1 * p(y = 1|\mathbf{X}) + 2 * p(y = 2|\mathbf{X})$$

8.5.1 New Dataset

You can change your dataset and find a different dataset or do more pre-processing like data augmentation and other processes on your data. Then, calculate the variance, check how new data change the variance, and check how this change can make the trained model better (Figure 8.9).

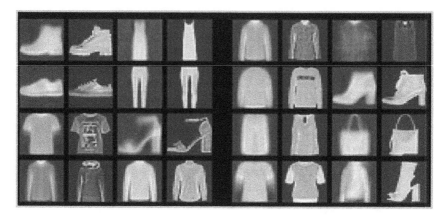

FIGURE 8.9 Different datasets or doing data preprocessing like data augmentation can change the variance.

8.6 BIAS/VARIANCE

Now let us see the relationship between bias and variance and how their values can be closed to the target. In total, there are four main states for the tradeoff between bias and variance (**L: Low, B: Bias, V: Variance, H: High**).

1. LB/LV

2. HB/LV

3. LB/HV

4. HB/HV

Figure 8.10 shows these four states. The question is, what is the noise value and its relations to these two parameters? Noises are a part of the data, and as mentioned in the first step, you can do some preprocessing on the data to remove or decrease the noise and then check some other reasons like the features or labels to see that they have been chosen correctly or not and do the right action. As you can see in Figure 8.10, the best state is LB/LV (Low Bias and Low Variance), that the values are very close to the target.

Another question is how we can find the best values for bias and variance? Figure 8.11 demonstrates the tradeoff between bias and variance and their relations to model complexity.

It corresponds to minimizing the total value that is equal to the summation of bias and variance. The dotted vertical line shows the point for optimum model complexity. The point in Figure 8.11 is the best value for

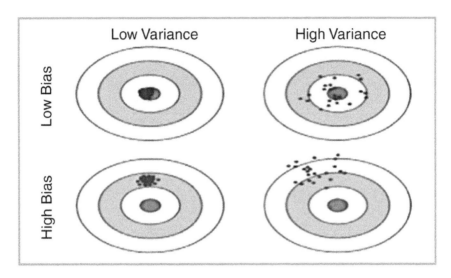

FIGURE 8.10   Bias/Variance changes.

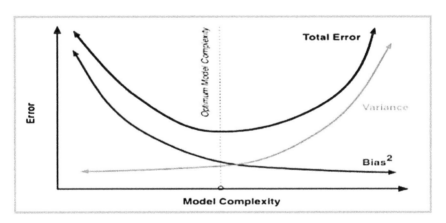

FIGURE 8.11   Bias/Variance tradeoff.

the total error. Thus, you can find the bias and variance values in your model and then find the point that the total error value starts to increase.

8.7 HOW CAN WE FIND THE PROBLEMS IN A MODEL?

Based on the previous discussion, after finding the bias and variance values and the relations between these two values, you should take the proper action based on values if the variance or the bias is high.

Figure 8.12 shows some graphs and the threshold that is the criteria for finding out the problem of the bad model and how you can improve it.

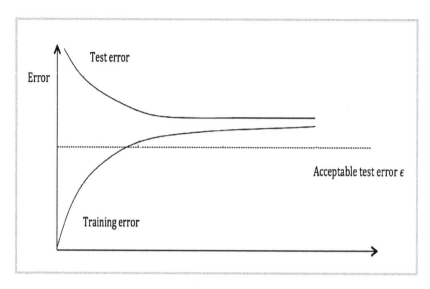

FIGURE 8.12   Testing and training error.

There are two states:

a. when the variance is high, and

b. when the bias is high.

The process is based on the training (or validation) error, test error, and acceptable (or target) error. So, in the first step, check the value of these two parameters and then follow the steps to find the reasons and solve them.

One discussion is about the high variance and high bias on the data. When the model has a small variance, and its bias is high, the model underfits the target, and on the other hand, a model with high variance leads to overfitting. Underfitting and overfitting are the problems that make the model inaccurate. To avoid these two problems, we can find the situations that make the model variance or bias high and then try to find the solution for these high values. Here we review these two situations.

8.7.1 High Variance

A high variance in the data happens when the data are very spread out from the mean value. When the variance is high, then in this situation, overfitting can happen, and to solve this problem at first, we should find the variance value and find that its value is high or not. For finding the high variance, you can look at:

1. training (or validation) error is lower than test error,

2. training (or validation) error is lower than an acceptable test error, and

3. test error is above the acceptable error.

After finding that the variance is high, you should know how to solve the problem and the solutions. Let us look at some solutions for it:

1. add more training data, or

2. reduce the model complexity, or

3. bagging.

As mentioned, these are the most popular solutions for the high-variance problem. However, there is still some active research in this field.

8.7.2 High Bias

When the prediction or classification is not correct, then the bias is high. When the data are very biased, then the concluding and final results are not correct. With high bias, underfitting can happen.

Based on Figure 8.12, the bias is high when this happens:

1. training error is higher than acceptable error

and you can solve it by:

1. increasing the number of features,

2. complex model or more in-depth, for example, the depth, and

3. boosting.

Bibliography

Allen, J., (1995). *Natural Language Understanding*, Benjamin/Cummings.

Alon, U., (2019). *An Introduction to Systems Biology: Design Principles of Biological Circuits*, CRC Press.

Ash, R. B., (1970). *Basic Probability Theory*, Wiley.

Bansal, A., and Ghayoumi, M, (2021). *A Hybrid Model to Improve Occluded Facial Expressions Prediction in the Wild during Conversational Head Movements*, INTELLI.

Bengio, Y., (1991). Artificial Neural Networks and their Application to Sequence Recognition. Ph.D. thesis, McGill University, (Computer Science), Montreal, Canada.

Bishop, C. M., (2006). *Pattern Recognition and Machine Learning*, Springer.

Bottou, L., (1991). *Stochastic Gradient Learning in Neural Networks, Proceedings of Neuro-Nîmes 91*, Nimes, France: EC2.

Chollet, F., (2018). *Deep Learning with Python*, Manning Publication.

Christian, S., Sergey, I., Vincent, V., and Alexander, A., (2017). An Inception-v4, Inception-ResNet and the Impact of Residual Connections on Learning.

Coleman, C., (2020). Selection via Proxy: Efficient Data Selection for Deep Learning, ICLR.

Delalleau, O., and Bengio, Y., (2011). Shallow vs. Deep Sum-product Networks, NIPS.

Deng, J., Dong, W., Socher, R., Li, L.-J., Li, K., and Fei-Fei, L., (2009). *ImageNet: ALarge-Scale Hierarchical Image Database, 2009 IEEE Conference on Computer Vision and Pattern Recognition (CVPR09)*, pp. 248–255.

Donahue, J., et al., (2015). *Long-term Recurrent Convolutional Networks for Visual Recognition and Description, CVPR*.

Dong, S., McKenna, S., and Psarrou, A., (2000). *Dynamic Vision: From Images to Face Recognition*, Imperial College Press.

Erhan, D., Bengio, Y., Courville, A., and Vincent, P., (2009). *Visualizing Higher-layer Features of a Deep Network*, University of Montreal, Vol. 1341.

Fei-Fei, L., Fergus, R., and Perona, P., (2006). One-shot Learning of Object Categories, *IEEE Transactions on Pattern Analysis and Machine Intelligence*, 28(4), pp. 594–611.

Ghayoumi, M., (2015). *A Review of Multimodal Biometric Systems Fusion Methods and Its Applications, 14th International Conference on Computer and Information Science*.

Ghayoumi, M., (2017). A Quick Review of Deep Learning in Facial Expression, *Journal of Communication and Computer*. doi:10.17265/1548-7709/2017.01.004

Ghayoumi, M., and Bansal, A. K., (2017). *Emotion Analysis Using Facial Key Points and Dihedral Group, International Journal of Advanced Studies in Computer Science and Engineering (IJASCSE).*

Ghayoumi, M., et al., (2006a). *Color Images Segmentation Using a Self-Organizing Network with Adaptive Learning Rate, International Journal of Information Technology*, Poland, pp. 72–80.

Ghayoumi, M., et al., (2006b). *Correlation Error Reduction of Images in Stereo Vision with Fuzzy Method and its Application on Cartesian Robot, 19th Australian Joint Conference on Artificial Intelligence (AI2006).*

Ghayoumi, M., et al., (2016a). A Formal Approach for Multimodal Integration to Drive Emotions, *Journal of Visual Languages and Sentient Systems*, pp. 48–54.

Ghayoumi, M., et al., (2016b). Follower Robot with an Optimized Gesture Recognition System, *Robotics: Science and Systems.*

Ghayoumi, M., et al., (2016c). The architecture of Emotion in Robots Using Convolutional Neural Networks, *Robotics: Science and Systems.*

Ghayoumi, M., et al., (2016d). *Emotion in Robots Using Convolutional Neural Networks, Eighth International Conference on Social Robotics.*

Ghayoumi, M., et al., (2016e). Multimodal Convolutional Neural Networks Model for Emotion in Robots, FTC.

Ghayoumi, M., et al., (2017). Facial Expression Analysis Using Deep Learning with Partial Integration to Other Modalities to Detect Emotion. Ph.D., Dissertation.

Ghayoumi, M., et al., (2018a). *Local Sensitive Hashing (LSH) and CNN for Object Recognition, ICMLA.*

Ghayoumi, M., et al., (2018b). Cognitive-based Architecture for Emotion in Social Robots, HRI.

Ghayoumi, M., et al., (2019). Fuzzy Knowledge-Based Architecture for Learning and Interaction in Social Robots, *Ai-HRI.*

Goodfellow, I., Bengio, Y., and Courville, A., (2016). *Deep Learning*, MIT Press.

Goodfellow, I., and Fridman, L., (2019). *Generative Adversarial Networks*, Artificial Intelligence Podcast.

Goodfellow, I. J., (2014). *On distinguishability criteria for estimating generative models*, In *International Conference on Learning Representations*, Workshops Track.

Graves, A., (2014). Generating Sequences with Recurrent Neural Networks, arXiv:1308.0850v5.

Graves, A., and Jaitly, N., (2014). Towards End-to-End Speech Recognition with Recurrent Neural Networks, ICML.

Hinton, G. E., (2007). *How to Do Backpropagation in a Brain*, Invited talk at the *NIPS'2007 Deep Learning Workshop.*

Hochreiter, S., and Schmidhuber, J., (1997). Long Short-Term Memory, *Neural Computation*, 9(8).

Hoon Ahn, B., (2020). Chameleon: Adaptive Code Optimization for Expedited Deep Neural Network Compilation, *ICLR.*

Hornik, K., Stinchcombe, M., and White, H., (1989). Multilayer Feedforward Networks are Universal Approximators, *Neural Networks*, 2.

Huszar, F., (2015). How (not) to train your generative model: schedule sampling, likelihood, adversary? arXiv:1511.05101.

Ioffe, S., and Szegedy, C., (2015). *Batch Normalization: Accelerating In-depth Network Training by Reducing Internal Covariate Shift*, ICML.

Jarrett, K., Kavukcuoglu, K., Ranzato, M., and LeCun, Y., (2009). *What is the Best Multi-Stage Architecture for Object Recognition? ICCV'09*.

Jastrzebski, S., (2020). *The Break-Even Point on Optimization Trajectories of Deep Neural Networks, International Conference on Learning Algorithms (ICLR)*.

Kaiming, H., et al., (2016). *Deep Residual Learning for Image Recognition, 2016 IEEE Conference on Computer Vision and Pattern Recognition (CVPR)*.

Karpathy, A., and Fei-Fei, L., (2015). Deep Visual-Semantic Alignments for Generating Image Descriptions, arXiv:1412.2306v2.

Karpathy, A., Johnson, J., and Fei-Fei, L., (2015). Visualizing and understanding recurrent networks, arXiv preprint arXiv:1506.02078.

Kennedy, J., and Eberhart, R. C., (1995). *Particle Swarm Optimization, Proceedings of the IEEE Conference on Neural Networks IV*, IEEE Service Center, New York.

Krizhevsky, A., (2010). Convolutional deep belief networks on CIFAR-10. Technical report, University of Toronto, Unpublished Manuscript: http://www.cs.utoronto.ca/kriz/conv-cifar10-aug2010.pdf.

Krizhevsky, A., Sutskever, I., and Hinton, E., (2012). *ImageNet Classification with Deep Convolutional Neural Networks, NIPS 12 Proceedings of the 25th International Conference on Neural Information Processing Systems*.

LeCun, Y., (1989). Generalization and network design strategies, Technical Report CRG-TR-89-4, University of Toronto.

LeCun, Y., Bengio, Y., and Hinton, G., (2015). Deep Learning, *Nature*, Vol. 521(7553). Nature Publishing Group.

LeCun, Y., Kavukcuoglu, K., and Farabet, C., (2010). *Convolutional networks and applications in vision, In Circuits and Systems (ISCAS), Proceedings of 2010 IEEE International Symposium on*, pp. 253–256. IEEE.

Leung, K. S., Jin, H. D., and Xu, Z. B., (2004). An Expanding Self Organizing Neural Network for the Traveling Salesman Problem, *Neurocomputing*, Vol. 62.

Maclaurin, D., Duvenaud, D., and Adams, R. P., (2015). Gradient-based hyperparameter optimization through reversible learning, arXiv preprint arXiv:1502.03492.

Martín, A., Paul B., Jianmin C., Zhifeng C., Andy D., et al., (2016). *TensorFlow: A System for Large-Scale Machine Learning, 12th USENIX Symposium on Operating Systems Design and Implementation*.

Merity, S., (2019). Single Headed Attention RNN: Stop Thinking with Your Head, https://arxiv.org/pdf/1911.11423.pdf.

Mingxing, T., and Le, Q. V., (2019). EfficientNet: Rethinking Model Scaling for Convolutional Neural Networks, https://arxiv.org/pdf/1905.11946.pdf.

Mitchell, T. M., (1997). *Machine Learning*, McGraw-Hill, New York.

Mnih, V., et al., (2015). Human-Level Control through Deep Reinforcement Learning, *Nature*, Vol. 518.

Mordvintsev, A., Olah, C., and Tyka, M., (2015). Inceptionism: Going deeper into neural networks, Google Research Blog.

Murphy, K. P., (2012). *Machine Learning: A Probabilistic Perspective*, MIT Press.

Nakkiran, P., (2019). Deep Double Descent: Where Bigger Models and More Data Hurts, https://arxiv.org/pdf/1912.02292.pdf.

Nesterov, Y., (2004). *Introductory Lectures on Convex Optimization: A Basic Course*, Applied Optimization, Kluwer Academic Publication.

Olshausen, B. A., Anderson, C. H., and Van Essen, D. C., (1993). A neurobiological model of visual attention and invariant pattern recognition based on dynamic routing of information, *The Journal of Neuroscience*, 13(11).

Pascanu, R., Mikolov, T., and Bengio, Y., (2013). *On the difficulty of training recurrent neural networks, ICML'2013.*

Quiroga, R. Q., Reddy, L., Kreiman, G., Koch, C., and Fried, I., (2005). Invariant visual representation by single neurons in the human brain, *Nature*, 435(7045).

Radford, A., Jozefowicz, R., and Sutskever, I., (2017). Learning to generate reviews and discovering sentiment, arXiv preprint arXiv:1704.01444.

Rockafellar, R. T., (1997). *Convex Analysis*, Princeton landmarks in mathematics.

Russel, S. J., and Norvig, P., (2003). *Artificial Intelligence: A Modern Approach*, Prentice-Hall.

Schmidhuber, J., (2015). Deep learning in neural networks, https://arxiv.org/pdf/1404.7828.pdf.

Simonyan, K., Vedaldi, A., and Zisserman, A., (2013). Deep inside convolutional networks: Visualising image classification models and saliency maps, arXiv preprint arXiv:1312.6034.

Simonyan, K., and Zisserman, A., (2015). *Very Deep Convolutional Networks for Large-Scale Image Recognition*, ICLR.

Srivastava, N., (2013). Improving Neural Networks with Dropout, Master's thesis, University of Toronto.

Sutskever, I., Martens, J., and Hinton, G., (2011). *Generating Text with Recurrent Neural Networks, Proceedings of the 28th International Conference on Machine Learning.*

Sutskever, I., Vinyals, O., and Le, Q. V., (2014). Sequence to Sequence Learning with Neural Networks, arXiv.org > cs > arXiv:1409.3215.

Szegedy, C., Liu, W., Jia, Y., Sermanet, P., Reed, S., Anguelov, D., Erhan, D., Vanhoucke, V., Rabinovich, A., et al., (2015). Going deeper with convolutions, doi:10.1109/cvpr.2015.7298594.

Taigman, Y. et al., (2014). *DeepFace: Closing the Gap to Human-level Performance in Face Verification*, CVPR.

Toshev, A., and Szegedy, C., (2014). DeepPose: Human Pose Estimation Via Deep Neural Networks, CVPR.

Uria, B., Murray, I., and Larochelle, H., (2014). *A Deep and Tractable Density Estimator*, ICML'2014.

Volodymyr, M., Koray, K., David, S., Andrei, A. R., Joel, V. et al., (2015). *Human-level Control through Deep Reinforcement Learning*, Macmillan Publishers.

Weston, J., Chopra, S., and Bordes, A., (2014). Memory networks, arXiv preprintarXiv:1410.3916.

Xu, K., Ba, J. L., Kiros, R., Cho, K., Courville, A., Salakhutdinov, R., Zemel, R. S., and Bengie, Y., (2015). *Show, Attend and Tell Neural Image Caption Generation with Visual Attention, ICML'2015*, arXiv:1502.03044.

Yan, H., (2020). *On Robustness of Neural Ordinary Differential Equations, ICLR.*

Ye, Ch., (2020). *Network Deconvolution, ICLR.*

Yosinski, J., Clune, J., Bengio, Y., and Lipson, H., (2014). *How Transferable are Features in Deep Neural Networks?, NIPS'2014.*

Zeiler, M., and Fergus, R., (2013). *Visualizing and Understanding Convolutional Networks, European Conference on Computer Vision*, pp. 818–833. https://arxiv.org/pdf/1311.2901.pdf

WEBSITES

https://colah.github.io/

https://cs231n.github.io/neural-networks-3/

https://github.com/meln-ds/Facial-Image-Generation-GAN

https://keras.io/api/utils/backend_utils/

https://probml.github.io/pml-book

https://towardsdatascience.com/comparative-performance-of-deep-learning-optimization-algorithms-using-numpy-24ce25c2f5e2

https://web.stanford.edu/~hastie/ElemStatLearn

https://www.bdhammel.com/learning-rates/

https://www.cs.cornell.edu/courses/cs4780/2018fa

https://www.cs.cornell.edu/courses/cs4780/2018fa/lectures/

https://www.python.org/

https://www.tensorflow.org/guide/

https://www.tensorflow.org/guide/

https://www.w3schools.com/python/python_intro.asp

Index

Milton Keynes UK
Ingram Content Group UK Ltd.
UKHW031535071024
449327UK00006B/153